"But it must be confest, 'tis so near to Heaven, that I dare not say it can be a proper situation for any but a race of mountaineers, whose lungs had been used to a rarify'd air . . ."

Daniel Defoe on Hampstead, 1724,
in *Tour through the Whole Island
of Great Britain*

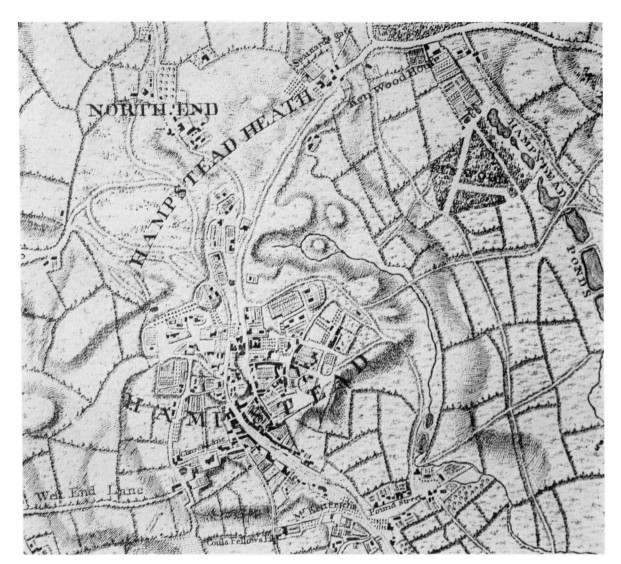

Section of John Rocque's map of 1746.

THE STREETS OF HAMPSTEAD

A New Survey of their Origins and Names, their Historic Houses and Notable Residents

by

CHRISTOPHER WADE

HIGH HILL PRESS
in association with
Camden History Society
1984

First published by the High Hill Press, 6a Hampstead
High Street, London, N.W.3. in 1972

Second Impression (corrected), 1973
Third Impression (corrected), 1976
Second Edition, Revised and Enlarged, 1984

Typeset in Times Roman by Herts Typesetting Services Ltd, Hertford
Printed in Great Britain by Hartnolls, Bodmin
ISBN 0 900462 21 3

CONTENTS

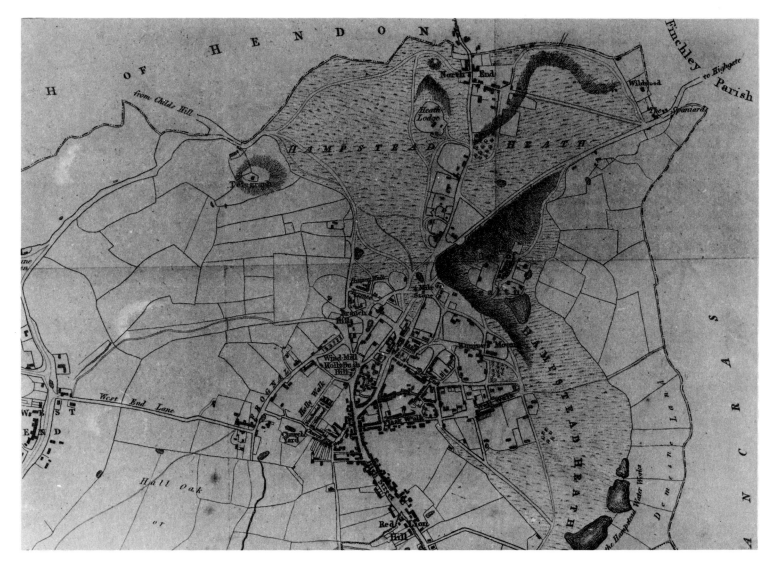

Section of J. and W. Newton's map for J. J. Park's *Topography and Natural History of Hampstead*, 1814.

ILLUSTRATIONS

Lower Heath Street (then Little Church Row) in 1886, before the Town Improvements.   *From a water-colour by Harold Lawes*   *Cover Picture*

MAPS

The cover picture and other illustrations are reproduced by kind permission of the London Borough of Camden's Local History Library

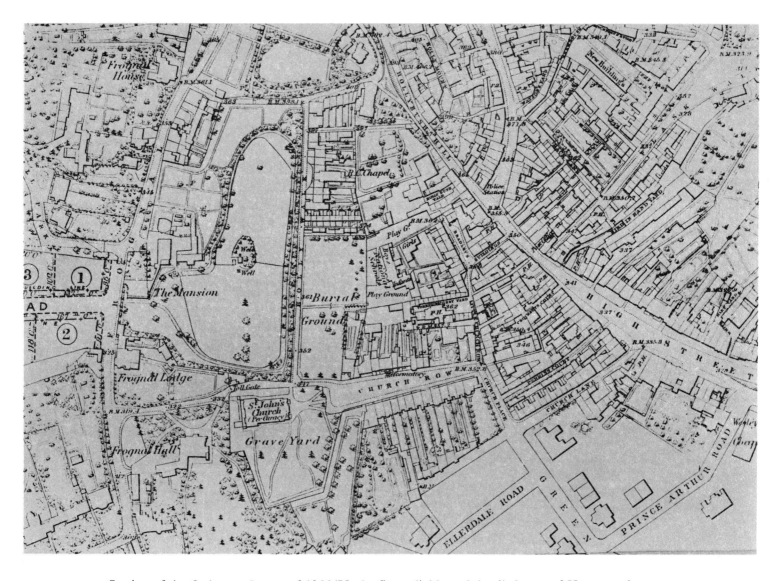

Section of the Ordnance Survey of 1866/75, the first reliable and detailed map of Hampstead streets.

INTRODUCTION

THE essential equipment for a local historian, said A. L. Rowse, is a strong pair of boots. A library can provide all sorts of persuasive topographical detail about a locality, but the only way of checking the facts is by walking the streets.

In 1970 I joined a group formed by Camden History Society to discover the origins of Hampstead street names. While digging into derivations, which involved Rate Books, Manor Minute-books, Street Directories and the extensive Local History Collection at Swiss Cottage Library, we unearthed a large number of fascinating facts about the streets concerned, especially about the houses and residents. Accordingly we began pounding the pavements of Hampstead, relating the archival evidence to the actual bricks and mortar and tarmac that we found in the streets. Finally, we wrote up our researches on a street-by-street basis and in 1972 produced the first edition of this walk-about history of Hampstead.

The present book is not just a revision but a complete rewrite of the original. It includes much new material that I have accumulated over the past decade (the group has long since disbanded), and eliminated a number of rather fuzzy facts and fancies that crept in before. Local history would be very dull without its myths and legends, and I have not removed the better traditional tales. I have, however, made it clear that they are only hearsay and I have excluded those stories which ought to be verifiable.

For instance, all the old Hampstead histories claimed that Wilkie Collins lived at 25 Church Row but, as no original records confirm this, he is back in my pending tray. Anyhow, there is no shortage of remarkable residents who definitely did live in Hampstead. As an earlier historian cried, 'Where shall the brilliant roll conclude?'

Rather than pure name-dropping, which some decry but enjoy just the same, I have tried to find out why the famous came to Hampstead and what they did while here: also what effect they had on the neighbourhood and *vice versa*. In the case of the artists and writers, who pepper these pages, I have explored their relevant works and noted some of their reflections of Hampstead. Constable's views of the Heath are well known, but not so D. H. Lawrence's short story set in Heath Street and Orwell's mockery of Willoughby Road. I have not included the many famous people who currently live in Hampstead for the sake of their peace and privacy.

There are so many dates of houses and residents that, for easy reading, these have sometimes been streamlined, e.g. 1950s rather than 1952–55. (Actual dates and sources are mostly available from me on request.) The dates of historic buildings have largely been taken from the Department of the Environment's Lists (see Sources). Where a range of dates is shown, I have given the latest (e.g. the parish church took three years to build, but I have dated it 1747). The age of old buildings is often difficult to determine, as so many houses have imported porticoes, bow windows and period bric-à-brac on their facades. Householders can be wildly wrong about the history of their houses and reminiscences of local residents can be madly misleading. Wartime memories are particularly suspect, as it is not always clear *which* war was involved.

More credit is paid in this edition to architects, thanks mainly to the publications of Sir Nikolaus Pevsner, who has made so many of us happily aware of architecture's subtleties. Andrew Saint's notes for the Victorian Society about Hampstead houses have also been most helpful.

There are many more commemorative plaques on local buildings now, thanks to Ralph Wade (no relation) and his Hampstead Plaque Fund. Most of his plaques are oval and black, while the official LCC/GLC plaques tend to be round and blue. Before the LCC scheme started in 1901, a number of tablets were erected by the Royal Society of Arts, generally in chocolate-brown terracotta.

Much of the research for the first edition of this book came from Shirley Harris, Brenda Tyler, Diana Wade and Wilfred Meadows, who was the admirable leader of the survey group. Help was provided, too, by Gillian Bebbington, the author of *London Street Names* (Batsford 1972). This new edition has benefited from the local researches carried out for the annual *Camden History Review*, which I launched for Camden History Society in 1973. Articles by Roger Ellis, Felicity Marpole, Christine Mill, Christopher Rolfe and Stephen Wilson have been especially helpful. Further information has been welcomed from Garth Andrews, Ruth Hall, David Hellings, Christopher Ikin, Alastair Service, David Sullivan and Philip Venning. The columns of the *Hampstead and Highgate Express* have, of course, been invaluable, as have Malcolm Holmes and his staff at Camden's Local History Library and my ever-collaborative wife.

As before, I must emphasise that this book can only be a personal selection of the material unearthed. The study of local history knows no end and finally depends on the sources and time available. Stendhal's awful warning on the subject, which we quoted in our first edition, remains true: 'It is terrifying to think how much research is needed to determine the truth of even the most unimportant fact.' May I beg my readers to help my terrifying researches by guiding me to the truth about Hampstead's dazzling history?

Hampstead   *Christopher Wade*
January 1984

HISTORICAL BACKGROUND

THE name Hampstead comes from the Old English Hamstede, meaning homestead or manor. There are Hampsteads—and variations like Hemel Hempstead—all over the country and in the old colonies. The Hampstead in New Hampshire (USA) was founded in 1749 and named 'in honour of the pleasant village in Middlesex County'.

The history of the manor dates back to a charter of AD 986, in which Ethelred the Unready gave the land to the monks of Westminster. The charter was almost certainly a forgery, but probably recorded an oral tradition for the gift and was necessary to establish the Abbey's title to the manor (there is a copy in the British Museum). According to this and other Anglo-Saxon charters, the boundaries of Hampstead were the same in the tenth century as they were nearly a thousand years later, when the borough was absorbed by Camden—from North End down to Primrose Hill, and from the Heath across to Kilburn High Road—approximately two thousand acres.

The manor was valued at only fifty shillings in the Domesday Book, and the picture it gives is of a small farm with a hundred pigs in a clearing of the vast Middlesex Forest. The farm belonged to the monks of Westminster throughout the Middle Ages, but they were not closely in touch. The only recorded visit of importance was during the Black Death, when Abbot Simon de Barcheston fled to Hampstead for his health, but he brought the plague with him and died here in 1349.

After Henry VIII's dissolution of the monasteries, the manor passed into lay hands, beginning in 1551 with Sir Thomas Wroth, a favourite of Edward VI. The first of Hampstead's absentee landlords, Wroth sold the property in 1620 to Baptist Hickes, later Lord Campden, the mercer and moneylender, who also owned land in the Notting Hill area and around Chipping Campden. Noted for their good works, his family founded a charity for the poor of Hampstead. So did the Earl of Gainsborough's family, who inherited the manor and donated some land around Well Walk. Their gifts are now united in the Wells and Campden Charity.

To complete the manor's history, it was sold to Sir William Langhorne in 1707, and passed by marriage to the Maryon, later Maryon Wilson, family. It was Sir Thomas Maryon Wilson who fought to the death to build houses on the Heath; he died in 1869. Though the manor as such is now defunct, a great-great-nephew of Sir Thomas still owns a large slice of Hampstead.

From Village to Suburb

Much of Hampstead's history is connected with its hill, its heath and its healthy air and water. There is a layer of Bagshot sand on the crest of the hill, a sand much prized and excavated over the centuries by the builders of

London. The sand explains both the heath, once more scrubby and gorsey than it is now, and the water supplies. The rain percolates the sand until it meets the top layer of clay, and then emerges as springs and streams, including three rivers—the Tyburn, the Westbourne and the Fleet. The first two are more or less 'lost rivers', but some of the early Fleet can be seen flowing on the Heath and filling the ponds. Hampstead was long famous for its pure water and a colony of laundresses was established here by the sixteenth century. It was said that rivermen on the Thames would look up at Hampstead and think it snow-capped, but it was really the linen left out to dry.

At the end of the seventeenth century, reports of the chalybeate (or ferruginous) well near Well Walk turned Hampstead into a spa. The fact that the water had such a peculiarly nasty taste must have contributed to its medicinal value, which was probably as real as the maladies of many who drank it. Though the popularity of the spa depended chiefly on day-trippers from London, boarding houses and villas were built for temporary residents and, when the popularity of the Wells died, about the same time that Queen Anne did, these houses were developed into permanent residences. By then, Hampstead had become known as a health resort and this was responsible for most of the fine new buildings of the eighteenth century.

After a second spa period later in the century, Hampstead was, according to its first historian, J. J. Park, 'the permanent residence of a select, amicable, respectable and opulent neighbourhood'. But in 1815, the year after Park's book was published, a visitor noted 'hundreds of mean houses and alleys'. Hampstead had grown too fast for general comfort. Another visitor in the 1870s remarked on 'Hampstead's narrow and dirty by-ways . . . and mean and crowded tenements'. Fortunately many of these were swept away by the Town Improvements scheme of the 1880s, which changed the face of upper High Street and lower Heath Street.

By then, the gap had been closed between Hampstead and the spreading city. In 1888 the village ceased to be in the Parish of St John, Hampstead, Middlesex, and officially became part of London. The first Hampstead Borough Council was formed in 1900, under the aegis of the London County Council, and was taken over by Camden Council in 1965. Hampstead has now lost its autonomy but is not without a mind of its own.

Street History

The discovery of some Roman pottery in Well Walk in 1774 supported the old theory that there was a Roman road across Hampstead Heath, but no firm evidence has been found. If the Romans used a route through central Hampstead as an alternative to Watling Street, when that low-lying track became waterlogged, it is probable that they used the main thoroughfare that exists today. Once a High Street, always a High Street.

Nearly all the routes on Rocque's map of 1746 (see frontispiece) have survived to this day, though many have changed in importance. For instance, Rocque suggests that Holly Hill, rather that Heath Street, was the main link between High Street and Whitestone Pond, but this was reversed by the early nineteenth century. Many early tracks led to wells and windmills, and the popularity of

Holly Hill may have derived from the two mills near its summit.

The first accurate map of Hampstead's streets was the Ordnance Survey of 1866, but this was before the development of the lower stretches of Frognal and Heath Street and of the Gayton, Willoughby and Redington Road areas.

The naming of streets was always a haphazard affair and, before the Penny Post of 1840, few of them had official titles. Names of landowners and pubs predominated, but the Victorians changed many of them to improve their image or because they preferred purely fanciful names. There are three Avenues near Redington Road called Rosecroft, Hollycroft and Ferncroft. Attempts to prove that a landowner called Mr Croft had three daughters called Rose, Holly and Fern have been in vain. It seems that the builder gave the roads pretty names to attract customers who would pay pretty prices.

Frognal Rise, about 1829, with Montagu Grove on the right. *Engraved from a drawing by William Westall.*

The Manor

THERE never was a Manor House in Hampstead nor, for that matter, a resident Lord of the Manor. But up to the last century there was a scatter of buildings at the junction of Frognal and Frognal Lane, which belonged to the Lord and, in particular, to his Manor Farm. Hereabouts was the earliest settlement of the hamlet of Hampstead, an agricultural huddle around the Frognal Brook and a sprinkling of village ponds.

With all this water around, the most likely of several explanations for the ancient name of FROGNAL is 'the place of the frogs'. (Quite a few other frog names scatter the country and Frognal also appears in Harrow and Chislehurst.) The ponds survived the building of some fine residences in upper Frognal during the Spa period but with the development of the lower end, which was not until the 1880s, all signs of farm life disappeared. Earlier in the century, a vicar of Hampstead was saying he preferred 'the open country of Frognal to the Town, a place pervaded with a sense of culture and sunshiny repose'.

Culture and repose are not obvious features of the Finchley Road end of Frognal but, in fact, Stephen Spender grew up in **No. 10** (now a part of **Heath Court**) and Home Office pathologist, Sir Bernard Spilsbury, found his final rest in 1947 at **No. 20** (part of an old-established hotel called Langorf, which is Frognal in reverse). Spender's autobiography, *World Within World*, described his home as an 'ugly house in the Hampstead style, as if built from a box of bricks', and recalled his walk up the 'hill of red-brick Frognal' to the local school. This was the Wren-style **University College School**, designed by Arnold Mitchell and built by Dove Brothers—or, as the Latin inscription in the entrance puts it, 'Redemptoribus: Dove Fratribus'. A new roof and fibreglass cupola, replicas of the originals, followed the terrible fire of 1978. A public school for boys, founded in Gower Street in 1830, UCS moved to this unpromising site in 1907. Among other problems, here was the source of the River Westbourne, which later heads for Kilburn and the Serpentine. The river still runs under the school in a specially-built crypt, where attempts have been made to grow mushrooms. The new building was opened by Edward VII, whose statue appears above the main door. Spenser Gate commemorates the fearsome headmaster at that time.

Opposite the school, there was much music-making in the 1950s. The opera-lovers of **Nos. 31 and 31A** combined their gardens to make Hampstead's Open Air Theatre (orchestra pit in one garden, stage in the other), and Dennis Brain and his horn were based at **No. 37**. The blue plaque on **No. 39** shows that Kate Greenaway died here in 1901. At the height of her fame as a children's book illustrator, she had the fashionable and locally-living Norman Shaw design her this studio house in 1885. It was bought in 1961 by Hampstead Borough Council. Her name lives on in nearby Greenaway Gardens, on an annual medal for children's book artists, and on a block in Boundary Road, but her grave in Hampstead Cemetery is, at this moment, sadly forgotten and forlorn.

Higher up, on the site of a Gothic pile called Frognal Priory, is **Frognal Close**, a neat but not gaudy group of houses designed in 1937 by E. L. Freud, son of Sigmund and father of Clement and Lucian. **Nos. 49 and 51** were built in 1895 by Sir Reginald Blomfield, architect of Lambeth Bridge and the Regent Street Quadrant. He lived in the upper house and Cobden-Sanderson, William Morris's typographical collaborator, in the other. Across the road, until the 1920s, was Priory Lodge, where Dr Samuel Johnson stayed and wrote most of *The Vanity of Human Wishes*. He resorted to Hampstead on several occasions between 1748 and 1752, mainly to give his neurotic wife a breath of country air. 'One man can learn more in a journey by the Hampstead coach,' he said, 'than another can in making the grand tour of Europe.' The design of **No. 66** by Connell, Ward and Lucas in 1938 caused a sensation. The architects, pioneers of the modern movement, appeared to be cocking a snook at their neighbour, Blomfield, who joined in a howl of local protest. Nonetheless, what was then called 'the greatest abortion ever perpetrated' has been hailed as the best pre-war modern house in England: it is also a Listed Building.

Further modern buildings can be seen in the unadopted road, FROGNAL WAY, which took over part of the Frognal Hall estate in 1924. Architectural historian Andrew Saint has called it 'the showpiece of interwar Hampstead housing', and certainly nearly every house has something of interest.

No. 4 has been typed by Pevsner as Hollywood Spanish-Colonial: note the curious 1934 plaque with what appears to be a flying monk. **No. 5** was by and for Adrian Gilbert Scott, grandson of Sir George, in 1930, and **No. 7** by Oswald Milne—the only architect to be Mayor of Hampstead? The Sun House, **No. 9**, by Maxwell Fry in 1935, has been much praised by modernists and is the only one of these houses to be listed. **No. 20** was designed in 1934 for Gracie Fields and her first husband, Archie Pitt and, keeping a low profile, **No. 22** is an ingenious in-fill by Philip Pank.

Back in Frognal, the centre part of **No. 94**, the Old Mansion, dates from about 1700. The wings were added in the last century in sympathetic style. The original garden stretched from Mount Vernon to Church Row, where a tollgate controlled access to Frognal. **Nos. 104 and 106** are dated c.1760, while **No. 108 and 110** go back to Queen Anne or earlier; they are among the oldest houses in Hampstead. In the eighteenth century they were joined together as a pub, variously called The Three Pigeons, Ye Pilgrim, The Windmill and The Duke of Cumberland. A niche for the pub sign can be seen on the north wall of No. 110, Grove Cottage, which now shows a plaque to its most distinguished resident, E. V. Knox, poet and *Punch* editor, who lived here from 1945–71. Should there not also be a plaque to his wife, Mary, daughter of E. H. Shepard who has achieved fame as illustrator of *Mary Poppins*? And perhaps another at No. 108 for the Diaghilev prima ballerina, Tamara Karsavina, resident here in the 1950s?

Frognal's other plaqueless stars of stage and screen

include Anton Walbrook at **No. 69** (he died there in 1967 and his ashes were deposited in the parish churchyard); and Anne Ziegler and Webster Booth at **No. 102**. But the magical contralto, Kathleen Ferrier, has her name on Frognal Mansions, **No. 97**, where she lived from 1942 until 1953, the year of her death. Among the mighty musicians who often climbed the fifty steps to her flat were Bliss, Barbirolli and Bruno Walter. Downhill from the Mansions is the charming old Bay Tree Cottage, **No. 95**, probably the gardener's cottage of the house behind (once Bay Tree Lodge), and **No. 79**, a late eighteenth-century house onto which was grafted a bigger building with Italianate watchtower, in 1902. Uphill is Frognal House, **No. 99**, dating from about 1740. After the Crimean War it was the Sailors' Orphan Girls' Home until 116 Fitzjohns Avenue was built for them in 1869. In the last war it became the home of General de Gaulle and his family from 1940–42, as the Hampstead Plaque confirms. The house was bought by the Sisters of St Dorothy in 1968 as an international finishing school for girls.

In a backwater from the main road is a delightful group of houses, **Nos. 103–109**, built by Henry Flitcroft about 1745. They were originally one house, Frognal Grove, centred on No. 105, with wings either side and a stables at No. 109. Flitcroft was architect of several London churches, including St Giles-in-the-Fields, and he had a street near there named after him; but his offer to design a new parish church for Hampstead was refused as he would not enter a competition for it. His Frognal house was sometimes known as Montagu House, as it was occupied by an eminent lawyer, Edward Montagu. It was later owned by Flitcroft's grand-daughter, who married into the Street family. G. E. Street, architect of the Law Courts in the Strand, enlarged the house in the 1860s. At this time, shortly after the residence here of Dr White, Vicar of Hampstead, the house was used for Baptist meetings. The southern wing had by then been hived off and became Upper Frognal Lodge.

The most famous occupant at No. 103 was Ramsay MacDonald, Britain's first Labour Prime Minister. His residence in this grand house from 1925–37 was much criticised by his socialist supporters, but he said he needed room for his vast library. MacDonald shares a plaque, not with his noteworthy son, Malcolm, a top Commonwealth administrator, but with Donald Ogden Stewart, an Oscar-winning screenwriter, who came here as a refugee for McCarthyism in the 1950s. If you saw Chaplin or Hepburn or Thurber calling at 103 Frognal, that was why. When put up for sale in the 1970s, the old stables at No. 109 included a 'Flitcroft fireplace', a heated pool and sauna, and a garage big enough for a Rolls. Offers for all this stabling were invited in the region of £97,500. **No. 111** was added to Frognal Grove in the late nineteenth century as a further coach house, but has also been upgraded to a desirable residence, with a fine array of metal sculpture out front. Montagu Grove was the name of this whole complex of houses and also of the approach road. The Lime Walk, planted here in the early eighteenth century, has featured in many old Hampstead pictures, notably in *As Happy as a King* by William Collins (father of Wilkie) at the Tate Gallery.

On the other side of Frognal, now the grounds of the Medical Research Institute, stood Hampstead's first workhouse, opened in 1729 in a derelict Tudor building (see *Camden History Review 4* for a graphic account). It survived until 1757 and some of the old house bricks are said to be incorporated in the present garden wall. A later, grander workhouse was built in New End, much to the relief of the superior fraternity in Frognal.

FROGNAL RISE consists of a house of that name, entered formerly from Frognal but now from Lower Terrace, and its two ex-stables, **Nos. 2 and 4**, converted into Spanish-style villas. Dating from the early nineteenth century, the house was enlarged and embellished with art nouveau in the 1880s. For many years it was the home of stockbroker Herbert Marnham, a leading local Baptist and philanthropist (see Grove Place). He was Mayor of Hampstead in 1925, received the freedom of the borough in 1934, and had an avenue named after him in West Hampstead.

OAK HILL WAY has two official signs at the Branch Hill end—'Private Road' and 'Footpath to West Hampstead'. It is, in fact, a very old right-of-way, but the only old house on it is **Combe Edge**, built in 1874. The red plaque shows that its original owner was Elizabeth Rundle Charles, author of a once-popular children's book with the formidable title *The Chronicles of the Schönberg Cotta Family*.

This rustic route leads to OAK HILL PARK, which was first developed around 1851 and won a Great Exhibition design award for gentlemen's dwellings. Most of the houses had gone by 1961, when the new development by Michael Lyell Associates won a Civic Trust Award. The oaks which once covered this hill were called North Wood, but they were cut down in 1470,

except for fifty trees, which the monks insisted be left. Few oaks remain today, but there is a block of flats called **Northwood Lodge** where Peter Sellers once lived. Gerard Manley Hopkins enjoyed climbing the trees when his family lived in Oak Hill Park in the 1850s, but the house has gone, as have the others where St Margaret's School originated, and where Sir William Rothenstein lived (see Church Row).

In the south-west corner, **Oak Hill House** is one of the two survivals and was one of several houses hereabouts visited by Florence Nightingale in search of fresh air treatment. **No. 1**, at the Frognal end, is also an original and during the 1930s was the home of publisher, Sir Geoffrey Faber. At this time another successful publisher, Sir Stanley Unwin, was living in Oak Hill Park and, undeterred by the bombs of the '40s, he stayed on until his death in 1968. After the war he bought the seven-acre estate from the Neave family—to avoid, as he said in *The Truth about a Publisher*, 'losing my house and my tennis court': he had **No. 4** built for himself beside the tennis court.

On the other side of Frognal is FROGNAL GARDENS, which was developed around 1890 over the garden of the Old Mansion. The main architect was James Neale, a pupil of G. E. Street, and the builders were the local firm of Allison & Foskett. **No. 20** was designed by and for Henry Ashley, who was to win the competition for Freemasons' Hall in the 1930s. His local architecture includes the Columbarium in the parish churchyard extension. Nearly invisible up a driveway, **No. 18** Frognal End, was built for Sir Walter Besant in 1892. There is an LCC plaque on the house to Besant, who also has a street named after him in West Hampstead. All of which goes to show that this forgotten novelist and antiquary was once somebody. The house was occupied in the 1920s by Lord Pentland, Governor of Madras, and from the 1940s by Labour leader, the Right Hon. Hugh Gaitskell. When Chancellor of the Exchequer in 1950, he even rejected 11 Downing Street in favour of 18 Frognal Gardens. Both Gaitskell and Besant are buried in the parish churchyard. Residents at **No. 16** have ranged from Sir Alexander Butterworth, Director of Welwyn Garden City Ltd. in the 1930s, to Bernice Rubens, Booker Prize winner in 1970. About this time, **No. 1a**, a Roman-style villa, was the home of financial wizard Sir Paul Chambers: his many achievements included chairmanship of ICI and the origination of our PAYE system.

FROGNAL LANE is the old route to the village of West End (round West End Green) and, until 1895, was included in West End Lane. The houses at the Frognal end are on the site of the old manorial buildings as the names suggest. The attractive **Nos. 19 and 21**, Maryon Hall and Maryon House, a semi-detached pair built around 1793, recall the Maryon Wilson family, Lords of the Manor since the eighteenth century. **No. 23**, Old Frognal Court, dating from 1785, has a plaque (not visible from the street) saying it was erected by Sir T. S. Wilson in 1785. Before it was much altered in the 1920s, the house was called The Ferns and belonged to the Prance family, great benefactors of Christ Church and St Stephen's.

In a side road opposite, **Hall Oak** uses the name of the Manor Farm on this site. The sturdy house was built for himself by Basil Champneys, which explains the lettering on the date plaque, 'AD 1881 BC'. Champneys was architect also of Newnham College and other Oxbridge buildings. His local contributions include Oak Tree House in Redington Gardens and two St Luke's churches, one in Kidderpore Avenue and one in Kentish Town. Nearby **No. 40**, Manor Lodge, was built about 1813 for the manorial bailiff. As late as the 1920s, the *Ham and High* was reporting that 'the summer meeting of the Court Leet and Court Baron of the Manor of Hampstead is held at Manor Lodge, Frognal'.

Branching off Frognal Lane, LANGLAND GARDENS first sprouted houses in the 1880s. **No. 21** has the distinction of being the birthplace of Cecil Beaton, photographer of the famous and designer, among other delights, of *My Fair Lady*. His family moved here in 1904, the year of his birth, because they 'considered the air so much healthier for growing children'. In *My Bolivian Aunt*, Beaton remembered this 'small, tall redbrick house of ornate but indiscriminate Dutch style', but preferred the grander house they moved to in Templewood Avenue in 1911. His memories of Heath Mount School in Heath Street were not altogether happy as another pupil, Evelyn Waugh no less, stuck pins into him. Waugh's *A Little Learning* records that he was suitably flogged for his crime.

Langland Gardens seems to be a fanciful street name but its neighbour, LINDFIELD GARDENS, built at the same time, commemorates a village on the Maryon Wilson estates in Sussex, not far from Nutley and Maresfield. **No. 15** was the first married home in the 1950s of Leon Garfield, now a leading children's author but then a biochemist at Whittington Hospital.

At the far end of Frognal Lane, **St Andrew's Church** has been a pillar of Presbyterianism since 1903. In fact, there has been a Presbyterian presence in Hampstead since 1662 and it dominated the early years of Rosslyn Hill Chapel. In 1844 the congregation rented the Temperance Hall in Perrins Court, on the site of the *Ham and High* offices, and in 1853 took over the old Long Room by Gainsborough Gardens. In 1862 they built Trinity Chapel in Willoughby Road and, exactly a hundred years later, they pulled most of it down and migrated to St Andrew's. They were united here with the Congregationalists in 1972. The junction with Finchley Road was where *The Woman in White* first met the hero of Wilkie Collins's novel, published in 1859. The recent television version could capture the remote rurality of this scene only by filming in deepest Suffolk.

To the north of Frognal Lane, three house-proud roads were developed early this century, including BRACKNELL GARDENS, which was named after a Maryon Wilson estate in Berkshire. **No. 16** was the home of Leonard Huxley until his death in 1933. He wrote a notable biography of his biologist father, T. H. Huxley, and also produced three famous sons, Julian, Aldous, and the Nobel Prizewinner, Andrew. Aldous was living here from 1917 until his marriage and consequent move to Hampstead Hill Gardens two years later. Sir Julian came to live in Pond Street in 1943. The eminent psychoanalyst, Melanie Klein, also spent her last years at No. 16, dying there in 1960. She specialised in children's unconscious and explored what Freud called 'the dim and shadowy era' of early childhood.

GREENAWAY GARDENS, which grew over the grounds of an estate known as Frognal Park around 1914, honours the memory of Kate Greenaway (see 39 Frognal). When the superstitiously-numbered **12a** was sold in 1970 to the Government of Trinidad and Tobago for its High Commissioner, it sported a heated log cabin in its extensive grounds. CHESTERFORD GARDENS, named after a Maryon Wilson estate in Essex, also covered part of Frognal Park. The pseudo-timbered **No. 18** was the last home of Henry Holiday, the artist (see Redington Gardens): he died here in 1927.

REDINGTON ROAD originated in 1875, when the Maryon Wilsons began selling off their Hampstead estates. The origin of the street name is unknown. It would be nice to think it commemorated the fourteenth-century Prior Redington, of the Order of St John, which held land near here (see Templewood Avenue), but it more likely salutes the distinguished Irish administrator, Sir Thomas Redington. The main developer, George Washington Hart, probably had Irish connections.

The houses at the Frognal end came first. **Nos. 2 and 4** were designed in 1876 by William Morris's associate, Philip Webb—'with quiet cleverness and curiosities' says Andrew Saint. The 'unrepentantly Gothic' **No. 6**, by T. K. Green was built as the vicarage of the Parish Church in the same year. Stained glass on the ground floor can be seen to include St John and a picture of the church. **No. 12** has a plaque on the side, giving its date 1878 and its original name, Wellesley House. **No. 16** is basically by Arts and Craftsman A. H. Mackmurdo in 1889, but extended by local architect Maxwell Ayrton in the 1920s. An early resident was Sir Hamo Thornycroft, sculptor of, for instance, the Boadicea on the Embankment. In the

1920s came civil engineer Sir Owen Williams, responsible for building Wembley Stadium and the M1, and in the 1970s actors John Alderton and Pauline Collins, responsible for modernising it upstairs-downstairs: they later sold it for about half a million.

On the opposite side, **No 35** was built by Horace Field (see 40 Rosslyn Hill) in 1887 and called Redington Lodge. In the late 1930s this was the home of LSE sociologist, Professor Morris Ginsberg. At the corner with Oak Hill Avenue, **No. 39** can be enjoyed for its fancy turret and the pargeted swans in its eaves.

OAK HILL AVENUE, originally Barby Avenue, has had two resident mountaineers of note—Christian Bonington and Elisabeth Schwarzkopf. The latter, who lived at **No. 3** in the 1930s with her husband, Walter Legge, is more famous for scaling the heights of opera, but mountaineering appears in her *Who's Who* list of recreations.

No. 45 Redington Road was frequently under attack by protesting mobs in 1962–64, when its occupant, Henry Brooke, was Home Secretary. Councillor Brooke rose from the Hampstead Borough Council in 1936, to the LCC in 1945, and to Parliament as Hampstead's Conservative MP from 1950–66. When Labour briefly won Hampstead in 1966, he left the area and became Baron Brooke of Cumnor. Higher up are two architecturally notable houses, **No. 81** by Sir Edward Maufe, designer of Guildford Cathedral, and the hilly **No. 87**, built in 1938 by Oliver Hill: 'good, asymmetrical, red brick villa in strictly modern forms', says Pevsner, who also logs the gardens by Christopher Tunnard.

Back on the east side, the quirky **No. 66** was built in 1910 by Dr William Garnett and given the jabberwocky name of The Wabe. He was an ardent fan of Lewis Carroll, as well as education adviser to the LCC, as well as grandfather to Hampstead's very own Boadicea, Peggy Jay.

Lewis Carroll was one of many distinguished visitors to **Oak Tree House** in REDINGTON GARDENS. Designed by Basil Champneys (see Frognal Lane) in 1874 for Henry Holiday, the house was originally approached from Branch Hill. This eminent Hampstead Victorian (see *Camden History Review 6*) specialised in stained glass—samples can be seen in Westminster Abbey and Rosslyn Hill Chapel—and established his own glassworks at 20 Church Row, where he claimed to have found the secret of fine blues in medieval glass. Apart form Carroll, who asked Holiday to illustrate *The Hunting of the Snark*, Gladstone came here to a Home Rule garden party, Sylvia Pankhurst to a suffragette meeting, and all the leading Pre-Raphaelites to discuss art. His wife, Catherine, was one of William Morris's chief embroiderers; his daughter, Winifred, was involved in the first performance in England of Schubert's string octet. All this, too, was in Oak Tree House, once a cultural centre, now highly desirable council flats.

TEMPLEWOOD AVENUE and GARDENS were laid out about 1910 and include some handsome houses by C. H. B. Quennell. This architect is perhaps more widely known as the author, with his wife Marjorie, of the series *A History of Everyday Things in England*. Another of their products was the writer, Peter Quennell. The streets were named after two local farms, Great and Little Templewood, which were probably once owned by the

Knights Templar. Cecil Beaton's family lived at **No. 1** Templewood Avenue, then called Temple Court, from 1911–22 (see Langland Gardens). Many houses in this area have become ambassadorial residences.

Quennell also designed many of the imposing houses in HEATH DRIVE, on the south side of Redington Road: this was first developed in 1890, under the more suitable name of West Hampstead Avenue. The lists of residents here bristle with Lords and Ladies and respectable establishment figures, so it may seem folly to make mention only of Thomas J. Wise, the greatest of all literary forgers. In 1910, when Wise came to **No. 25**, his book collection was considered supreme, but in 1934 many were revealed as forgeries. The typographer, Stanley Morison (see Hollyberry Lane), was instrumental in unmasking him. After Wise died here in 1937, his Ashley Library, forgeries or no, was sold to the British Museum.

KIDDERPORE AVENUE was laid out in 1890, mostly over the carriageway to the stately **Kidderpore Hall**, which has survived at the top of the hill. The original hall (architect: T. Howard) was built in 1843 by John Teil, an East India merchant with tanneries in the Kidderpore district of Calcutta. The northern part of his estate was bought in the 1850s for a reservoir, and the rest acquired by **Westfield College** in 1890. The college, which originated in Maresfield Gardens in 1882 as the Girton of North London, became part of London University in 1902 and admitted male students from 1964. Of the few buildings here, old and new, *not* now owned by the college, **No. 14** has a delightfully quirky facade. This includes an S for artist George Swinstead, who built the

house in 1901. Since the last war, it has been the home of the musical Craxton family. Harold Craxton and his daughter Janet, the oboeist, taught for many years at the Royal Academy of Music: they created the Craxton Memorial Trust and the Craxton Prize to help young musicians.

St Luke's Church next door was built in 1896, with a touch of Arts and Crafts, by Basil Champneys (see Frognal Lane). Note the ox on the weathervane, which is St Luke's logo. At the other end of the avenue, **No. 7** was for many years the home of James Gunn RA, painter of many official portraits, including George VI and our present Queen: he died here in 1965. Opposite his house, **No. 4** is surprisingly tudorised and splendidly decorated with grotesques and other mouldings. The date 1900 is on the front and the colourful tympanum over the corner door must not be missed. Cinema pioneer Jonas Wolfe lived here in the 1940s.

KIDDERPORE GARDENS originated in the 1890s, but was called Cecilia Road until about 1907. St Margaret's School came to **No. 18** from Oak Hill Park after the last war. The school was founded in 1884 'for the daughters of gentle people', which later included Sir Gerald du Maurier's daughters, Angela and Daphne.

PLATT'S LANE was named after Thomas Pell Platt, who about 1840 built Child's Hill House on a site near the junction with Rosecroft Avenue. Platt was an oriental scholar and his main claim to fame was translating the Bible into Ethiopian. This cannot have contributed much to the enormous house, grounds and farm which he owned, and where he died in 1852: the estate was sold up at the turn of the century. **No. 8** is now the most interesting house in the road, being a characteristic long, low building by C. F. A. Voysey, a pioneer of the Modern Movement. He built it for his father in 1896 (date on drainpipe) and it was, says Pevsner, 'astonishingly ahead of its date'. The original name, Annesley Lodge (one of Voysey's Christian names was Annesley), is barely visible on the west wall. **Nos. 14 and 16** are marked 'West Middlesex Waterworks 1806', but the date has been corrected below to the more likely 1875, which is when the huge reservoir was built here. Opposite, **No. 21** has a private plaque to Thomas Masaryk, first president of Czechoslovakia, who lived here in exile during World War I and planned the liberation of his country. Platt's Lane was once known as Duval's Lane, after a notorious seventeenth-century highwayman, and this name was later corrupted into Devil's Lane. Bible-thumping Mr Platt put an end to all of that.

FERNCROFT, HOLLYCROFT and ROSECROFT AVENUES had their names officially approved in 1896, and the streets were developed over the meadows of Platt's Farm by the busy builder, George Hart. It was he who devised these fanciful names. A tributary of the River Westbourne (see UCS, Frognal) rises near here and crosses Ferncroft Avenue close to where **Croftway**, an old right of way, leads down to Finchley Road. As a literary curiosity, the writer Gilbert Cannan, one-time secretary to J. M. Barrie, stayed at the decorative **No. 25** in 1916–17, after his marriage to the one-time Mrs Barrie had broken up and his health had broken down.

In Hollycroft Avenue, **No. 46** was designed in 1907 by Sir Guy Dawber, noted for his houses in the Cotswolds and Hampstead Garden Suburb. **No. 28** was the last home of Leslie Brooke, father of Henry and illustrator of the popular *Johnny Crow* series: he died in 1940 and would have been glad to know that he was buried by the local undertaker, J. Crowe. Quennell appears again in Rosecroft Avenue at the heavily shuttered **No. 20**, Croft House, which he designed in 1898. The same date can be seen in the eaves of **No. 18**, together with some naked nymphs: the sculpted facade of **No. 17** is also worth viewing. Cartoonist Gerald Scarfe was living at the turreted **No. 1** in the 1960s.

West of Platt's Lane, BRIARDALE and CLORANE GARDENS were also creations of George Washington Hart. The former name seems to be merely fanciful but the latter, not being euphonic, may commemorate a country seat of that name in Limerick.

At the north end of the Lane, TELEGRAPH HILL is named after the signalling station based here during the Napoleonic wars. Originally serving the Duke of York's headquarters, the station became a vital link between the Admiralty and Yarmouth from 1808–14, using a shutter semaphore system. The present road was built in the 1930s, and those who remember pianist and composer, Billy Mayerl, will like to know that he had a house here in the 1940s called Marigold, the title of one of his hits.

Round the corner, WEST HEATH ROAD follows a very old track from Hampstead village to Child's Hill. At the corner with Platt's Lane is the imposing **Sarum Chase**, 'unashamedly Hollywood Tudor' said Pevsner. It was built in 1932 for artist Frank Salisbury (hence Sarum) by his nephew Vyvyan, and was much frequented by royalty and politicians for portrait sittings. When Salisbury died in 1962, he left the house to the British Council of

Churches as a 'centre for Christian gatherings'. This proved 'impractical': it is now St Vedast's School for Boys. In contrasting style, **No. 9** by James Gowan is, some say, 'one of the finest modern houses in Hampstead'. Between here and Branch Hill, an area being much redeveloped, was until recently The Grange, once the home of the flamboyant actor-manager, Beerbohm Tree. He abandoned it in 1891 because of the problems of getting transport to 'such a remote country spot'.

The Grove

THE emblem of the old Hampstead Vestry, forerunner of the Borough Council, was a sprig of holly and the west side of HOLLY HILL had a grove of hollies until the 1940s. But in the eighteenth century this road was called Cloth Hill, which suggests that some of the many local laundresses were hanging out their washing on the holly bushes. Certainly the road follows an ancient track, much lowered over the years by digging from surrounding sandpits. The raised path has old railings and bollard posts dated 1828.

Behind the western wall is the Junior Branch of **University College School** (see Frognal), established in 1891, sixteen years before their seniors came to Hampstead. Their original building, dating from 1665, was demolished in 1927, but its outline has been preserved in an ornamental garden. Its front door, staircase and some panelling have also been incorporated in the new school. Among the staff here early this century was the poet, James Elroy Flecker: he started the library but was otherwise not a success. On the same side, **Nos. 15–19** have been converted from an early eighteenth-century farmhouse. Tradition has it that this was connected with one of the windmills of Windmill Hill, and that part of it was the granary. Confusingly, **Nos. 12 and 14** are jointly called Granary House, for reasons unknown: this early nineteenth-century building has been used by builders, sheet metal workers and, in the 1920s, as Holly School, a

rival preparatory school to UCS. The picturesque houses, **Nos. 16–24** are basically early to mid nineteenth-century with later additions, such as the sundial. The garages higher up are eighteenth-century bricked vaults, linked with the houses in Holly Mount and supporting their gardens. Before the age of the car, they were used as workshops, a greengrocer's and a florist's.

The name HOLLY BUSH HILL used to include all Holly Hill as well, but now embraces only a grassy triangle and five handsome houses. **No. 1**, Alpine Cottage, is early nineteenth century, but the others are mid or late eighteenth century, some with spear-and-pineapple railings. White and weather-boarded, **Romney's House** has a blue plaque to salute the artist's residence here. This was originally the stables of a house in The Mount behind, which Romney bought in 1796. But his efforts to convert them into a house, studio and Palace of Art broke his health, and in 1799 he returned to his neglected wife in Kendal.

In 1807 the building was enlarged for Assembly Rooms, with money raised by a tontine lottery, and became a cultural centre for Hampstead, the Burgh House (q.v.) of its day. Here was held in 1829 the first Heath Protection meeting, chaired by James Fenton of Fenton House, and here in 1833 was given a notable series of lectures by such authorities as Faraday, Constable and Elizabeth Fry. In the 1880s, when the new Town Hall in

Haverstock Hill had taken away the assembly business, first the Liberals, then the Constitutional Club moved in. This continued until the 1920s, when the last beneficiary of the tontine died and the house could be sold. From 1929 until the war it belonged to Clough Williams Ellis, architect of Portmeirion, who had it 'much altered and adapted to our curious habits', as he wrote in *Architect Errant*: he also added the urns on the gateposts.

Around 1900 Holly Bush Hill was planned as the Hampstead station on the proposed Charing Cross, Euston and Hampstead Underground Railway. Powers were sought to widen approach roads and also open stations on the West Heath. Protesters put a stop to that idea.

Round the corner in HOLLY MOUNT, the **Holly Bush Tavern** was also converted from stables and, from 1807, was linked with the Assembly Rooms, originally as their catering wing. Many of the houses in this extraordinarily complex cul-de-sac are eighteenth-century, but the street name is not used in the Rate Books until the 1830s. Earlier, this jumbled area came under the heading of 'Nagg's Head Side', after the pub in Heath Street. The 1851 Census showed a good social mix here, including eleven servants and four laundresses.

Nos. 1 and 2 were then one house, occupied by the octogenarian Lady Mary Bentham, sister-in-law of Jeremy, together with some family, a maid, a cook, a housekeeper, and her own laundress. Under the gardens of **Nos. 3 and 4** are the eighteenth-century arched vaults, mentioned in Holly Hill. **Nos. 5–8**, recognisable on the 1762 Manor Map, are early examples of back-to-back housing. **Nos. 14 and 15** are mid eighteenth century. Dame

Anna Neagle was living at No. 14 in the late 1930s. The nearly invisible **No. 16**, once Alma Cottage, is partly built on top of a house in Golden Yard. **No. 17** was the first Baptist Chapel in Hampstead, built in 1818. In 1860 it became the printing works of the *Ham and High* (see Perrins Court) and later the *Hampstead Record*, and from 1911 it has been an artist's studio. Note the weathervane on **No. 18**, which was a beer shop in the 1830s, the Holly Mount Laundry in the 1850s, and a lodging house at the turn of the century. Holly Bush House, **No. 21**, was the home for many years of Donald and Catherine Carswell, close friends of D. H. Lawrence, who liked to lodge here. Donald, a barrister, checked *Women in Love* for libel: Catherine helped type *Lady Chatterley's Lover*.

Of the two eastern exits from Holly Mount, the further one is anonymous, though once identified as Cock Alley for convenience: the other is the attractive **Holly Bush Steps**, which lead down to GOLDEN YARD. The name of this pleasant backwater does not appear in the Rate Books until 1831, being previously given as Gouldings Yard. The Goulding family owned much property hereabouts. The yard's history, going back to the sixteenth century, has been traced by a local resident and summarised on a display board here. **No. 4** is the house supporting 16 Holly Mount (see above): the occupant of the former had once to complain to the latter about coal falling through into his attic.

Off Heath Street, THE MOUNT has many eighteenth-century houses and two major artistic connections. The first is Romney's residence (see above) at **No. 6**, Cloth Hill. This was built as two houses in 1694, the year after Fenton House, but was rapidly made into one dwelling.

As the daughter of the house married Andrew Pitt, who is known to have entertained Voltaire in Hampstead, it seems likely that the great philosopher came here. The house was divided again in 1801 and, at the end of the last century, the main part (old No. 5) was the family home of publisher Edward Bell; the remainder was The Mount School. The garden wall and gate, which are DOE listed, can be seen in Ford Madox Brown's famous picture, *Work*—the street's other claim to artistic fame. (Versions of the painting are in Manchester and Birmingham galleries, and one is reproduced with commentary in *Camden History Review 2*.) The Pre-Raphaelite Madox Brown began the picture in 1852, inspired by seeing navvies at work on Hampstead's main drainage. **No. 11**, Caroline House, and **No. 12**, Holly Cottage, are also visible in the background of *Work* and Madox Brown lodged at the latter in 1883, when recovering from violent gout. Before this time, No. 11 belonged to Mrs Margaret Money and this enclave off The Mount, including the attractive **St Helen's Cottage**, became known as **Money's Yard**.

On the 1835 map, the north end of the street is shown as Mount Pleasant and the south as Elba Place. The 1851 Rate Book called the whole road Silver Street (this stayed until 1936), and THE MOUNT SQUARE was known as Golden Square. Caroline White commented sourly on all these precious titles in 1903: 'There is nothing in their present appearance except irony to suggest the etymology of the names.' But fortunes have changed and the square is no longer the slum that Daphne du Maurier described in one of her family biographies. **Nos. 7 and 8** were respectively the laundry and the stables of Old Grove House, to which there is a gate marked 1859. **Nos. 10–16** are eighteenth-century, the last one being used by a veterinary surgeon and later a farrier, right up to the Great War. Note the horseshoe on the gate.

Across Hampstead Grove is the so-called ADMIRAL'S WALK. Originally included in The Grove, the street was given its present name in 1949 to connect with its main residence, **Admiral's House**, dating from 1700. Until very recently, this was thought to have been the home of the eighteenth-century Admiral Matthew Barton. But, as an article in *Camden History Review 9* revealed, he was living in Rosslyn Hill all the time: and the highest naval rank associated with the house was a mere lieutenant. It was Lieut. Fountain North who lived here from 1775 to his death in 1811 and adapted the roof to look like the deck of a ship; he even installed a couple of cannons up there, which he fired to celebrate naval victories. The residence here of architect-extraordinary, Sir George Gilbert Scott, is well authenticated by the official plaque. During his stay here (1856–64) he was working on plans for the Albert Memorial, and he also designed a gallery for the local Christ Church. It is a curiosity that this champion of Gothic Revival, and the only begetter of St Pancras Station Hotel, should have taken this sober-sided house, and that the dreaded restorer should not have left his mark on the building. Among other eminent occupants here have been the army historian, Sir John Fortescue, who was ironically the first to call it Admiral's House, and his wife Winifred, author of *There's Rosemary, There's Rue*. One of Constable's three paintings of this house is at the Tate Gallery.

Grove Lodge, attached to Admiral's House, is of about

the same age, and also bears an official plaque. This notes that John Galsworthy lived here from 1918 to 1933, his years of fame. During this time he completed *The Forsyte Saga*, and in 1932 he won the Nobel Prize for Literature. As he was too ill to collect his prize, a delegation came to Grove Lodge to deliver it. Behind is a picturesque Gothic villa of early nineteenth-century origins called **Terrace Lodge**. Here the street ends and so surely must its present name, though Lieutenant's Walk is not nearly so impressive.

In his *Table Book* of 1827, William Hone called Hampstead 'the place of groves', and so it has remained. There are still enough fine old trees in HAMPSTEAD GROVE to justify the name. From its first mention in the Rate Books of 1831, it was just 'The Grove', and the name sometimes embraced parts of Upper and Lower Terrace, as well as Admiral's Walk and even Admiral's House. To avoid confusion with The Grove in Highgate, the name was changed to Hampstead Grove in 1937.

Towards Whitestone Pond, a grassy bank conceals Hampstead's first **reservoir**, built in 1856 by the New River Company: a nautical weathervane floats above it. Here also is the Meteorological Station and **observatory** of the Hampstead Scientific Society, which is open on some Saturday nights for star-gazing.

Among the neo-Georgian houses to the south, **No. 32** was recently the home of Lord Cottesloe. His chairmanships have ranged from Tate Gallery to Battersea Dogs' Home, and his name is well known at the National Theatre. Nearby is **New Grove House**, of the eighteenth century but 'stuccoed and tudorised', as Pevsner put it, around 1840. Here, as the red plaque shows, lived the writer and artist, George du Maurier, from 1874 to 1895, the year before his death. His grand-daughter, Daphne, has written much about his life and there is some autobiographical detail in his novels, *Trilby* and *Peter Ibbetson*. The latter includes scenes in Hampstead, as did du Maurier's famous *Punch* cartoons. Adjoining is the early eighteenth-century **Old Grove House**, with the highest roof terrace in London. When the garden front was rebuilt in the 1950s, all old windows blocked up by (presumably) the window tax were carefully re-blocked in identical fashion.

Across the road is the oldest surviving mansion in Hampstead, **Fenton House**, built in 1693. The date was found on a chimney. Early in the eighteenth century, this was called Ostend House and was owned by a silk merchant, Joshua Gee. His initials appear on the remarkable wrought-iron gates by Tijou, giving on to Holly Bush Hill. Gee had close connections with the American colonies, traded with George Washington's father, imported pig-iron from Maryland and was an original Pennsylvania mortgagee. In 1793 the property, then known as The Clock House (see dial over door), was bought by Philip Fenton, a Riga merchant, who left it to his nephew, James. The latter added the loggia and new entrance on the east side. Fenton House, together with its beautiful contents and garden, was bequeathed by Lady Binning in 1952 to the National Trust, and should be visited for its pictures, porcelain and furniture, as well as the Benton Fletcher collection of musical instruments. There is even a 1612 harpsichord once used by Handel.

On the east side of the Grove are six attractive cottages, **Nos. 4–14**, nearly two hundred years old but unlisted.

Thirteenth-century tiles have been found in the basement of one cottage, and praying shells, as used by medieval travellers, in the walls of another. Could these have been lodgings for Westminster monks visiting their Hampstead estate? Two leading artists of the London Group lived in this row for many years—Brian Robb at No. 10 and Ethelbert White at No. 14. Mary Webb came to No. 12 in 1923, enjoying some scant literary success, but frequently unwell and unhappy. Among other things her husband, Henry, a master at King Alfred's, was having an affair with a pupil. She completed *Precious Bane* here in 1924, but it was not until three years later, after praise from the Prime Minister, Stanley Baldwin, that the book finally brought her fame—and in that same year she died. The success of *Precious Bane*, however, allowed Henry to give up teaching and marry his pupil.

Across the green of Holly Bush Hill is MOUNT VERNON, named after General Charles Vernon, an aide-de-camp to George III, who owned land here around 1800. The eighteenth-century **Mount Vernon House** is linked with the building which looms rather too large beside it, now the **National Institute for Biological Standards and Control**. This pseudo-château by Roger Smith began in 1880 as the North London Hospital for Consumption, the healthy air of Hampstead having influenced the location. The building was much enlarged over the years, including a western extension by local architect Maxwell Ayrton: he also designed the main block at Mill Hill, whither the hospital went before the Great War. It is now in Northwood, but is still called Mount Vernon Hospital. From 1914 until quite recently, the Hampstead building became the National Institute for Medical Research. Among its distinguished directors living here have been physiologist Sir Henry Dale, now commemorated with a blue plaque, and immunologist Sir Peter Medawar, of whom C. P. Snow said: 'If he had designed the world, it would have been a better place.' Each of these directors shared a Nobel Prize for Medicine.

The attractive terrace of cottages, **Nos. 1–6**, dates from 1800. Note the GH and coronet on the rainwater-head of No. 1, thanks to Sir Geoffrey Harmsworth, the press baron, who lived here in the 1930s. **Mount Vernon Cottages** date from about 1820, and the same period applies to **Abernethy House**, originally built as a parochial school for girls. This had become a lodging house by 1873, when Robert Louis Stevenson (see plaque) paid the first of several brief visits. His fellow-lodger was (Sir) Sidney Colvin, then Slade Professor of Fine Art at Cambridge, who thought Hampstead would be a cure for the young writer's bad lungs, depression and drugs. Before leaving Mount Vernon, note the three old lamp posts, which are listed, and the fire insurance plate on No. 6, a reminder that up to about 1870 fire brigades were for subscribers only.

There are more nineteenth-century lamp posts in HOLLY WALK (for derivation see Holly Hill) and, on a clear day, there is a breathtaking view across the Parish Church to south London. On the west side is **Moreton**, a rough-cast house designed by Thomas Garner in 1896 (date on drainpipes), for art-lover Frederick Sidney, FSA. His initials and crest are over the porch and his belief that 'God is Al in Al Thinges' (*sic*) is over the door.

Opposite is the splendid terrace called HOLLY PLACE, built in 1816. **No. 9** has a Hampstead plaque to show that this was the Watch House for the new police force from 1830. The barred cellar was probably used as cells. Since those days the Hampstead police have gone literally, but not rapidly, downhill. By 1834 they moved to the foot of Holly Hill, where the clock tower building now stands. By 1870 a new police station was opened on the west side of Rosslyn Hill, but in 1913 this was abandoned for the present site at the corner of Downshire Hill. **Nos. 10 and 11**, which are technically in HOLLYBERRY LANE, are thought to have been connected with the old Watch House. No. 10 may have been the sergeant's house and No. 11 the stables. Around 1939, composer Sir William Walton was living in the former, and compositor Stanley Morison in the latter. Morison was a type-setter only in the artistic sense, for in the 1930s, among other achievements, he redesigned *The Times* and transformed its *Literary Supplement*. He also used his genius in typography to expose the master-forger, Thomas Wise (see Heath Drive).

The centrepiece of Holly Place is **St Mary's Church**. This is one of the earliest Roman Catholic churches in London, and takes its dedication from the old parish church before its rebuilding in 1747. The congregation grew around Abbé Morel, who settled in Hampstead in the 1790s, along with other refugees from the French Revolution: he died in 1852 and was buried in the porch. Two years previously, the belfry facade was added, together with the Virgin and Child copied from an Argentinian statue. (The original church, being built before the Catholic Emancipation Act of 1829, had a discreetly plain front.) Inside is a portrait of Morel, painted by Clarkson Stanfield, and a Byzantine baldacchino by Adrian Gilbert Scott. Among worshippers here in the last war was another notable French refugee, General de Gaulle. **No. 4** is now the Presbytery (originally at No. 8). **No. 1** became St Vincent's Orphanage and School in 1872, but closed in 1907 through lack of funds.

Lower down the hill are two culs-de-sac. BENHAM'S PLACE has nine terraced cottages, built in 1813 by William Benham, who was also a grocer and cheesemonger in the High Street. The road name does not appear in the Rate Books until 1829. The curious semi's of PROSPECT PLACE, stuccoed in front and weatherboarded behind, date from the 1790s and are painted delightfully in pink and pistacchio. There is a tradition that they were built by French refugee settlers, or even by Abbé Morel himself. Writer Paul Jennings lived at **No. 4** in the 1950s, oddly briefly. The prospect over the churchyard extension is decidedly pleasing.

Back in Holly Bush Hill, a terrace of old houses facing the green marks the beginning of WINDMILL HILL. An early seventeenth-century print shows the hill of Hampstead crowned with two windmills, and the sites have been noted in Holly Hill and Hampstead Grove. The Victorian novelist and Hampstead lover, Beatrice Harraden, found this area 'as picturesque as old Blois itself and lived in by sweet presences'. In the four houses here, all dating from about 1730, the longest, if not sweetest, presence must have been that of Joanna Baillie, the Scottish literary lioness. She lived at **Bolton House** from 1791 until her death in 1851, and was one of the first women to be commemorated with an official plaque. Her *Plays on the Passions* may now be forgotten, but they caused a sensation in the 1790s, and in the following years her house was much visited by Byron, Wordsworth, Keats, and especially by Sir Walter Scott. As the latter said in *Marmion*, 'Avon's swans think Shakespeare lives again', so he gave her a scarf brooch and she knitted him a purse. In the 1930s, a rich artist called Miss Gluck lived at Bolton House and had Sir Edward Maufe design her a studio, complete with minstrel's gallery, at the bottom of her garden: this is now **No. 7.** Charles Bean King built **Nos. 1–6**, which have their dates 1894/5 under their eaves. Virginia Woolf was a frequent visitor to No. 5 in Edwardian times, as she was taking Greek lessons there from the formidable feminist, Janet Case. The student later recalled 'How I went hot and cold going to Windmill Hill'.

Where the road ends at the Heath is the romantic eighteenth-century cottage, **Capo di Monte**, previously called Upper Terrace Cottage or Siddons Cottage. In the absence of a plaque, an S over the door recalls that the great actress Sarah Siddons stayed here in 1804–5. As with so many visitors, she came to Hampstead for her health, 'for the strong air and quiet surroundings', but particularly to be near a doctor using the latest electrical cure for rheumatism. She doubtless also called on Joanna Baillie, in whose play *De Monfort* she had recently starred at Drury Lane. Her other great success was as Lady Macbeth, so much so that the play always ended with her sleep-walking scene. No wonder Mr Evans the draper in Hampstead High Street was so alarmed when she examined some material in his shop and demanded dramatically, 'Will it wash?'

In the 1940s Sir Kenneth Clark lived briefly in Capo di Monte, but he found the house too small: larger guests like Oliver Lyttelton filled the entire dining room, he complained in *The Other Half.* So he moved across the lane to UPPER TERRACE and found more elbow room in **Upper Terrace House.** This eighteenth-century mansion had been much altered in the 1930s, mainly by Oliver Hill, and Clark found the staircase 'hideous' until it proved to be solid enough to make the ideal air raid shelter. After the war, when the house was overrun by his wife's fashion shows, he tended to work, he said, in a car parked in a cul-de-sac near Ken Wood. So they moved to Saltwood Castle in Kent. After Sir Kenneth came Sir Leon Bagrit, sometimes called 'the father of British automation': he stayed in the house until 1976.

The street takes its name from **the terrace** of houses to the west, dating from about 1740, which has been variously divided up into two, three or four residences. For much of the nineteenth century, this was the home of the philanthropic Jackson brothers, who built New Court, off Flask Walk (q.v.) as model dwellings for workers. Hugh Jackson, a solicitor, also accommodated his father-in-law, Sir William Beechey, the portrait painter, who died in Upper Terrace in 1839. Hugh's son, Thomas, became an architect, who in 1883 redecorated the Parish Church chancel. Another remarkable resident here in the 1880s was Canon Alfred Ainger, Queen Victoria's chaplain and a local eccentric. He was a great friend of George du Maurier (see Hampstead Grove), and supplied him with ideas and captions for his cartoons—including the immortal *Curate's Egg*, published in *Punch* in 1895. Du Maurier's portrait of Ainger is now in the National Portrait Gallery. The house at the west end is **Upper Terrace Lodge** which, apart from having Florence Nightingale on its guest list, had the distinction of being extended in the 1920s by Sir Edwin Lutyens.

LOWER TERRACE is also named after a pretty row of late Georgian houses, but of humbler stature. **No. 2** was one of Constable's homes in the summers of 1821 and 1822. He came mainly for his wife's health, for his letters show that he was dying to get back to his big canvasses in his Charlotte Street studio. During his time in Lower Terrace, he produced a large number of oil sketches of the area, notably of the Heath and of Admiral's House, but also of the shed in his back garden and the family washing on the line. This cottage was recently offered for sale at £159,950. **No. 10**, Netley Cottage, invisible behind its wall, dates back to 1779, and may have been a farm house. At the Whitestone Pond end of the road is **Hawthorne House**, once called Tudor House, now a convalescent home. The garden is on the site of what was once the Speakers' Corner of Hampstead and here, under a beech tree, preached Wesley and Whitefield and other famous orators. The original house was built by Ernest George and Peto in 1882 for W. J. Goode, whose fortune was in Goode's China Shop in South Audley Street (it is still there): he filled the house with art treasures. He also bought the garden adjoining his house, which used to belong to Upper Terrace House and was linked to the latter by a tunnel. The ridge of this tunnel (now closed) can still be seen in the lane running between the two houses.

This Lane leads to JUDGES WALK, which is not really a road, as it has no houses, but it is still remarkable for its name, its view and its donkeys. Variously called Prospect Walk, King's Bench Avenue and Upper Terrace Avenue, it became Judges' Walk earlier this century. The traditional reason for its name is that, during the Great Plague of 1665, judges came here to hold the assizes. Historians who challenge this theory say that its name probably derives from nearby Branch Hill Lodge, once known as Judges' Bench House. Anyway, all agree that the view from here over Hendon and Harrow is spectacular. Constable has captured it in many of his paintings, though not all of them turn out to be quite accurate. Several of them, however, such as *Hampstead Heath with a Rainbow* (1836), do include donkeys, and it would be nice to think that they are related to the beasts of burden who carry children round the Judges' Walk area today.

BRANCH HILL, which was an old branch route to Child's Hill, also appears in many Constable views, especially its pond. This, with artistic licence, varies in size from a horse pond to a miniature Buttermere. The pond dried up early this century, but its true outline can still be seen near the junction with West Heath Road. Opposite the pond site, **The Chestnuts**, now a men's hostel, for most of the 1930s was the home of the Negro bass, Paul Robeson. After his great success in *Show Boat*, especially with the song *Ole Man River*, he was lionised in Hampstead by a distinguished crowd, including his near neighbour, Ramsay MacDonald.

To the north is the **Spedan Tower estate**, currently sprouting blocks of flats. John Lewis, the store owner, built a vast house here (now gone) and died there in 1928 aged 93: his middle name was Spedan. The site was bought by Camden Council in 1972 for £328,000, and sold by them nine years later to a private developer for over two million pounds. This would by no means have paid for the Council's own development nearby at SPEDAN CLOSE. The forty-two semis built in 1978 in the grounds of **Branch Hill Lodge** have been called the most expensive Council houses ever built. Their foundations were largely the problem as the site, which was remote and on a steep slope, had particularly bad soil excavated from the Northern Line at the start of the century. The average cost of the houses, ingeniously designed by Gordon Benson and Alan Forsyth (and others), was about £70,000.

The original Branch Hill Lodge was known in the early eighteenth century as Bleak Hall, as well as Judges' Bench House. Since then the place has had many associations with lawyers. The house was redesigned in 1745 by Henry Flitcroft, then based in Frognal, for Sir Thomas Clarke, Master of the Rolls. After him came Sir Thomas Parker, a fraudulent judge, and Alexander Wedderburn, a crafty Lord Chancellor. Wedderburn, who became Earl of Rosslyn (see Rosslyn Hill), was known as 'the second Judge Jeffreys' for his harsh treatment of the Gordon Rioters. On his death, George III remarked, 'He has not left a greater rogue behind in my dominions'; on hearing which Lord Thurlow said he was glad to know that the King was at least temporarily sane. The only other resident of note here was Lady Byron, who rented the house shortly after her separation from the poet. The present house is partly by S. S. Teulon about 1868, but rebuilt in 1901 (this date is on it). It was bought by the Council from Lord Glendyne in 1965 and, complete with new wing, became an old people's home. **The Gardens** is the name of the Lodge's Gothic gatehouse and bears its date—1868. This was also designed by Teulon in the same flamboyant style that he used for St Stephen's, Rosslyn Hill.

SECTION THREE

The Wells

IN 1698, six swampy acres around WELL WALK, 'being about certain medicinal waters', were given to the poor of Hampstead by the Gainsborough family, then Lords of the Manor. The Wells Trust was formed and an entrepreneur was found to take a twenty-one year lease of the land to develop it into a spa. A Long Room was quickly built, opposite the present **drinking fountain**, a Victorian monument to the Gainsboroughs' gift. The Long Room was about eighty feet long, and embraced a small Pump Room, where the chalybeate water was dutifully drunk, and a large Assembly Room, where patients could recover and be entertained. Dancing, cards and concerts were organised (see *Camden History Review 3*). Between the Long Room and the Tavern was a row of raffling booths.

Unfortunately, Hampstead Wells became too popular with the wrong sort of people and, as early as 1709, their riotous assemblies were the subject of lawsuits by local residents. By 1721, the Spa had such a bad name that the lease was not renewed: the Long Room surprisingly became a chapel of ease to the Parish Church. In the 1740s, when the church was being rebuilt, the whole congregation converged on the Well Walk chapel. With the building of Christ Church in 1852, the old Long Room again became vacant, but was soon filled by a Presbyterian congregation, until they built their chapel in 1862 in Willoughby Road. After some years as a Drill Hall for Hampstead Volunteers, it was finally demolished in 1882.

A second Long Room and a Ball Room were built in Well Walk in the 1730s, when attempts were made to revive the Spa. These buildings, on the site of **Wells House**, next to Burgh House (see New End Square), were designed more for residents than for visitors. Even so, Pope, Johnson and Mrs Thrale were among the distinguished visitors, as well as Fanny Burney, whose heroine in *Evelina* wrote about the horrors of an evening at Hampstead Wells. After the eighteenth century, the second Spa buildings were turned into residences, but they were badly bombed in the last war and, despite much protest from preservationists, demolished in 1948. In their stead rose the sixty-four Council flats of Wells House, with the north-east wing on the Ball Room site and the south-east wing on the Long Room site. The architect C. H. James designed the blocks to harmonise with Burgh House, so much so that the Queen Anne house is nearly lost in their midst. Owing to a post-war timber shortage, the roof had to be made of steel. The design won the RIBA's London Architecture Bronze Medal in 1949.

Across the road, **No. 2** was the home in the 1970s of the artist Barbara Jones, author of the delightful *Follies and Grottoes*, and **No. 12** was Max Beerbohm's temporary lodging in the first World War. The plaque on **No. 14** gives

Well Walk, 1879, showing the Spa's first Long Room three years before it was pulled down. *From a water-colour by J. P. Emslie.*

many claims to fame for Marie Stopes, the pioneer of birth control, but does not say when or why she came to this house, or that her marriage in 1911 to R. R. Gates was a disaster. She came in 1909, mainly to get away from her mother in Denning Road (q.v.), and from her traumatic experiences in Well Walk she produced her best-selling *Married Love*. That versatile actress, Fay Compton, lived in **No. 22** in the early 1930s, having just successively played principal boy in panto, Ophelia to Godfrey Tearle's *Hamlet*, and the lead in Dodie Smith's *Autumn Crocus*. **No. 26** was the last Hampstead home (1926–35) of Margaret Llewelyn Davies, champion of the Women's Cooperative Guild. She fought especially for the rights of married women 'tied to the washtub', and Leonard Woolf described her as 'a kind of Joan of Arc to her cohorts of housewives in her crusade against ignorance, poverty and injustice'.

Near the fountain, **No. 13** was the home of Poet Laureate John Masefield in 1914–16, but the blue plaque salutes H. M. Hyndman, who died here in 1921. Hyndman was influential in the formative years of the Labour Party and has been called the 'classic top-hatted socialist'. The handsome **Manaton Lodge**, No. 19, was converted from the gardener's cottage in the grounds of Foley House and named after the owner's village in Devon. **Nos. 21–27**, also in the old Foley House garden, were built by Henry Legg in 1882 for Edward Gotto of The Logs (q.v.); his initials are on the gateposts. Until 1924, this impressive row of houses was known as Foley Avenue. In the 1920s and 30s Maxwell Garnett, son of William (q.v.) and General Secretary of the League of Nations, lived at No. 21, and in the early 1930s, just after

the success of *The Good Companions*, J. B. Priestley had his first London home at No. 27. The **seat** at the north end of Well Walk has replaced Keats's Seat, where this notable Hampstead resident was seen by antiquarian William Hone 'sitting and sobbing his dying breath into a handkerchief'.

Across the road, the elaborate **No. 50**, variously known as Thwaitehead (see plaque) and Klippan House, was built in 1881 by and for architect Ewan Christian: the date is on the wall and his initials on the weathervane. The ornate lamp bracket, dated about 1600, was brought by him from Nuremberg. An inscription, now obliterated, round the cornice read: 'God's Providence is mine Inheritance'—which was particularly apt for this successful church architect. Christian designed St Saviour's, Eton Road, gave a font to St Stephen's, and added the north aisle to Christ Church: he was also co-architect of the National Portrait Gallery.

At the entrance to Gainsborough Gardens, **Wellside** has a tablet recording the site of the old Pump Room. In the 1960s this was the home of economics expert, Lord Balogh, properly Baron Balogh of Hampstead. **No. 46** is early eighteenth-century, with delightful Gothic features added later. They must have pleased Temple Moore, another distinguished church architect, who lived here from 1892–1921. Among the first residents at **No. 40** were the Constable family, as the blue plaque shows. On their arrival in 1827, the artist wrote ecstatically to his friend, Fisher, 'We are at length fixed in our comfortable little house in Well Walk . . . Our little drawing room commands a view unsurpassed in Europe.' Tragically his wife, Maria, died here the following year, but this remained his family home—he had seven children—until his death in 1837. This was also the home before the first World War of Charles Weekley, Relieving Officer of Hampstead, whose son had the misfortune to marry Frieda von Richthofen. It was at 40 Well Walk that Frieda dumped her two daughters in 1912 before eloping with D. H. Lawrence. Lovers of Sturge Moore's poems and engravings will want to know that he lived here in the 1930s.

Nos. 38 and 36 are also early nineteenth-century, with porches added later, but **Nos. 34 and 32** are an early eighteenth-century pair. E. V.Knox (q.v.) lived at No. 34 from 1922 to 1945, and a **seat** on the other side of the road commemorates him. Before the First World War H. N. Brailsford, the Socialist writer, lived at No. 32. During the war it belonged to poets Dollie and Ernest Radford, and it was here that D. H. Lawrence and Frieda found refuge in 1917 after eviction from Cornwall as suspected spies. The visit is vividly described in Lawrence's *Kangaroo*. Film star Leslie Banks, also a notable Captain Hook in *Peter Pan*, lived here in the 1930s and complained that the ghost of Keats used to turn on all his bath taps. The site of the postman's house, where Keats lodged with his dying brother, Tom, is now under the **Wells Tavern**. This pub replaced The Green Man in 1850, which itself replaced The Whitestone. The publican in the 1920s was Sidney Strube, better known as a *Daily Express* cartoonist.

GAINSBOROUGH GARDENS covers the pleasure grounds of the first Spa, which included a bowling green to the north and an ornamental pond in the middle. The outline of the latter can be seen in the central **lawn**, which J. B. Priestley (q.v.) and others would remember as a tennis court. In the northern shrubbery there is still an **ice house**, presumably a souvenir of the Long Room's catering department, but this is not viewable. What can be seen is the nearby **bell-turret**, salvaged by a local resident from Trinity Church in Finchley Road. The Gardens were laid out by the Wells Trust in the 1880s, after its plan to run a road through the middle of them brought violent protest. A petition was launched to use the site for 'aged, infirm and poor artists and literary men', but this failed. The overall planner and architect of about half the houses was Henry Legg: these include the gardener's **lodge**, dated 1886. **Nos. 11–14** were by Horace Field in the early 1890s. **Nos. 3 and 4**, by E. J.May in 1883, were said to be the first houses with hot air heating: you can still see a sliding panel on the side of No. 4, designed to let out excess heat.

At the top of Well Passage is WELL ROAD, which in Spa times led to the head spring and bath pond. This was on the site of **Nos. 6–8**. In these houses, earlier this century, lived three great pioneers in different fields. No. 6 was the home of (Sir) Ian MacAlister, the radical reformer of the Royal Institute of British Architects. No. 7 housed the statistician, Karl Pearson, who has just earned a blue plaque here; and in No. 8 lived the Egyptologist, Flinders Petrie, whose blue plaque went to his later home in Cannon Place (q.v.).

Nos. 17–20 are in The Logs, the name of which is as inexplicable as its style. Andrew Saint notes its 'wonderful uncertainty between Gothic and Italian', while Pevsner had no doubts about calling it 'a formidable atrocity'. The obscure architect responsible was J. S. Nightingale, who built it in 1868 for an even obscurer civil engineer called Edward Gotto, who died here in 1897: his initials appear

New End in 1890, showing cottages (now demolished) at the foot of Christchurch Steps. *From a water-colour by J. Appleton.*

elaborately on the Cannon Lane side of the house. At some period, a gateway labelled Lion House was added (did it come from the old zoo?). In 1951, the house was converted into maisonettes, one of which was occupied in the late 1960s by pop-eyed comedian Marty Feldman, who much enjoyed, he said, this cock-eyed house. A contemporary occupant of **No. 22**, the Logs Cottage, was Graham Reynolds, V & A art and Constable authority.

Cannon Cottage and **Providence Corner** date from the early eighteenth century. The former, once called Holly Hedge Cottage, was the home of Daphne du Maurier and her husband in the 1930s. In the southern stretch of Well Road, **No. 1 Wellmount Studios** bears a plaque to Mark Gertler, who painted here in 1932/33, but who spent many more years in Rudall Crescent (q.v.). As in the case of Flinders Petrie, the plaque has gone to the more prominent place.

Behind the studios is GROVE PLACE, of which **Nos. 29–31** were clevely converted from the Bickersteth Hall in 1970. Topped by a couple of cupolas, the hall was built for Christ Church in 1895 and named after its famous vicar, who became Bishop of Exeter. Confusingly, an 1871 St Pancras plaque and an 1886 Jubilee plaque, attributed to Mrs Edward Gotto, have beeen added to the building, along with a tiny Roman centurion in cricketing pose. Across the road are twenty-eight 'model dwellings for artisans', or **Grove Place Flats**, built about 1914 on the site of the Spa's Bath House by local Baptist benefactor, Herbert Marnham (q.v.).

WHITE BEAR PLACE is a non-street behind the pub, Ye Olde White Bear (see New End). Adjoining it is the non-rectangular NEW END SQUARE. This was developed during the Spa period, the grander **Nos. 16–20** being early eighteenth-century and the lesser houses a little later. The entrance to No. 20 is wisterically pretty. **No. 40**, with the Tuscan portico, was built in 1759 as the Hawk Tavern and rebuilt in 1815 after a fire. It had become the highly respectable Rose Lodge when Tennyson installed his mother here in the 1860s, and it was linked by a hole in the wall with 75 Flask Walk (q.v.), where his sister lived. From 1932, this was the home of artist and Slade tutor George Charlton: a sample of his work is in Burgh House. Stanley Spencer was a frequent visitor here during the last war, and his portrait of Mrs Charlton is in the Tate.

This area suffered heavy bombing during the war and the beautiful **Burgh House** was lucky to survive. Built in 1703, it soon became the residence of the Spa physician, William Gibbons: his initials are on the ornate wrought-iron gates. The Rev. Allatson Burgh, who lived here until his death in 1856, was an unpopular vicar of St Lawrence Jewry in the City, but he should be remembered locally as one of the protestors in 1829 who helped prevent the Lord of the Manor building on the Heath. From 1858 to about 1881, Burgh House was the headquarters and Officers' Mess of the Royal East Middlesex Militia, with additional buildings nearer Well Walk, and barracks in Willow Road. Later residents included Thomas Grylls, of the famous stained glass painters, Burlison and Grylls; Dr George Williamson, art expert extraordinary and adviser of Pierpont Morgan among others; and Elsie Bambridge, daughter of Rudyard Kipling. After the last war, the house was bought by the local Council and started a new career as a community centre. From 1979 it has been leased to the Burgh House Trust, who run it as Hampstead's meeting place, exhibition centre and local history museum.

At the corner with FLASK WALK, with a dignified Doric portico is Rose Mount, **No. 75**, dating from 1812. Captain Richard Jesse, RN, who lived here in the 1860s, married Tennyson's daughter, Emily, and nobly accommodated his mother-in-law in the adjoining house (see above). The studded **doors** in the wall opposite came, according to oral tradition, from Newgate Jail. Along the street is the nucleus of another village **green**, which was large enough in 1712 to hold Happy Hampstead's first recorded fair. More permanently on the green were the village stocks and the Watchman's hut, complete with two overnight cells. All we have now is the **Baths** building, designed by Henry Legg in 1888 for the Wells and Campden Charity, but recently converted into town houses. There are two sorts of **Flask Cottages** nearby—old ones with twisted chimneys and the 1950s variety, ingeniously devised by a Council architect. Next door is **Boade's Mews**, converted from a garage belonging (surprisingly) to High Close in Holford Road: Boade's Corner was the old name for this area.

Here also is MURRAY TERRACE, a name first found in the 1840 Rate Book, probably derived from William Murray, Earl of Mansfield, who had many local connections, including Ken Wood. On the other side of Flask Walk, GARDNOR ROAD was developed in 1871/2 in the grounds of **Gardnor House**. The names come from Thomas Gardnor, whose family owned a large slice of central Hampstead, and who built the house about 1736. The grand Gardnor tomb in the parish churchyard

(near the main gate) has recently been restored. Other residents in the house have included local historian G. W. Potter and, very recently, Kingsley Amis and Elizabeth Jane Howard.

Back in Flask Walk the pleasant terrace, **Nos. 53–67**, was also built by Thomas Gardnor, in 1811. The Hampstead Subscription Library started at No. 65 in 1833, with Constable among the founder-members. To the south is LUTTON TERRACE, an alley seen on the 1814 map. Lutton is a common English place-name, but has no obvious local association. At the end of the alley is **New Court**, two blocks of forty 'model dwellings' erected by the philanthropic Jackson brothers of Upper Terrace (q.v.). The old name, New Buildings, can be seen on a faded sign. The main block was built in 1855 and the smaller one, with a reading room, in 1871. A war memorial stone shows that fifty residents went off to World War I, 'of whom ten died for the good cause'. From the 1960s there have been plans to demolish and redevelop these blocks, but they are still alive with short-life housing.

Most of **Nos. 35–47** Flask Walk are early nineteenth-century workers' cottages, and so is **No. 48** across the road, 'with a good cast iron head knocker' noted in the DOE Listing. LAKIS CLOSE was designed in 1973 by Gerson Rottenberg for a Greek Cypriot developer, who named it after his son (Lakis, pronounced 'lackeys', is short for Michael). Also modern and meritorious are **Nos. 30–36** Flask Walk, replacing the Salvation Army barracks and a Montessori school.

The Flask is a listed pub, though this version dates only from 1874. The original Lower Flask Tavern, which gave this old street its name, was the place where Spa water was once bottled for sale in the City. The water could be bought in Fleet Street at threepence a flask, and customers were earnestly advised to beware of imitations. In Richardson's novel of 1748, *Clarissa*, the Lower Flask was described as 'a place where second-rate persons are to be found occasionally in a swinish condition'. Much has changed since then, including the pub sign, which now pictures the wrong sort of flask. At the High Street entrance to Flask Walk there used to be a two-storey superstructure like the one in Perrins Court: this fell down in 1911, but the roofline is still visible. In 1973 the Council created a pedestrian-preferred **precinct** here (though cars still intrude), and won a Civic Trust Award for it. Of the old shops, **Nos. 1–7** are basically early eighteenth-century, and **Nos. 2 and 4** early nineteenth-century: the latter has preserved its original shopfront.

BACK LANE is called Garden Place on the 1862 map, and part of it is Alfred Terrace in the 1888 Directory, probably after Lord Alfred Paget, who owned land here. As in Flask Walk, many of the workers' cottages have been taken over by brainworkers, but some industry survives at the **Radius Works**, once a jobmaster's stables, now a display contractor. Down a minute alley next door are **Keil's Cottages**, which once connected with Mr Keil, a baker in the High Street (on the Tube Station site).

At the top of the lane, the straitened STREATLEY PLACE wanders off towards New End. Called Brewers Lane in the eighteenth century, and Brewhouse Lane in the nineteenth, the present 'deliberately neutral' name was chosen in the 1890s to improve its image, according to the GLC Street Naming Section. **Streatley Flats** were built in the early years of this century by the benevolent Herbert Marnham (q.v.). There is a myth that MANSFIELD PLACE was built for the police, with constables in the cottages and the sergeant-in-charge in the house at the end. Equally unsupported is the theory that this pleasant backwater is named after Lord Mansfield of Ken Wood, but this is quite likely. It is also probable that the houses were built in early Victorian times, and practically certain that the land was previously a nursery garden.

Back in Streatley Place, the date of **New End Primary School**, 1906, is clearly seen. The building of the school was encouraged by the Education Act of 1903, and the LCC architect was T. J. Bailey. Like UCS in Frognal, this is another school with a river running through its foundations, in this case part of the Fleet. At the corner with New End, the **School House** was once a beer shop called The City Arms.

The name NEW END appears in the local burial register for 1696, so some of this development pre-dates the Spa. The 'end' here means outer district, like Hampstead's North, South and West Ends, which shows that the original colony of cottages was on the outskirts of the village. None of these has survived, but **No. 30** is listed as early eighteenth-century, with flush-framed windows. (Later, all window frames had to be recessed from the wall face, as a fire precaution.)

Nearly all the houses in the lower stretch of New End started in some sort of trade, which explains their wide windows. The 1899 Directory shows a dairy, a baker, a chimney sweep, a farrier and, at **No. 57**, a fried fish shop. Over this corner shop can be seen the name Southwell

Terrace, which applied to this side of the street only. On the building opposite, **No. 16**, is a plaque commemorating the dispensary and soup kitchen erected here in 1853, by voluntary contributions. This was done as a thank-offering for the parish being spared from the 'noisome pestilence', a cholera plague: the architect was R. Hesketh and the chief instigator was Hampstead's vigorous vicar, Thomas Ainger. This Provident Dispensary, which offered cheap medicine to the poor, and a pint of soup for a penny, was made redundant in the 1940s and converted into an architect's office in 1955, at which time the plaque was salvaged from the waiting room.

Nos. 10–14, which are listed as a group, date from 1725. **New End Hospital** is not listed and the dating is complicated. Hampstead's second workhouse (see Frognal for the first) opened on this site in 1800, but a new building, now the central block, was erected about 1845. The water tower and the unusual circular wards at the back (architect: Charles Bell) were added in 1884. The uphill extension came in 1905, designed by Keith Young and Henry Hall. Apart from the workhouse, the main building was used as Hampstead's Town Hall until the grand new one was built on Haverstock Hill in 1877. The whole institution became a Military Hospital in 1915, and has stayed a hospital ever since. A back room with a grilled window is said to be the place where the workhouse men broke stones for road-mending before they got their breakfast: the stones had to be broken small enough to pass through the grille.

Opposite the hospital, the **Duke of Hamilton** is the latest version of an alehouse mentioned in the Manor Survey of 1762. The cobbled alley at the side once led to the stables.

The building next door began life as a mortuary in 1890, but has been the **New End Theatre** from 1974. A number of productions and managements have died since then—but the shows go happily on. Further downhill are the Council flats, **Carnegie House** (architects: A. and J. Soutar), named after Hampstead's first lady Mayor, wife of the Vicar of the Parish Church, and opened by her in 1948. **Ye Olde White Bear** used to show its 1704 foundation stone, but it has been much rebuilt since then. The open space towards Christchurch Hill was once known as White Bear Green.

CHRISTCHURCH HILL is shown as Green Man Lane on the 1862 map, named after a pub on the site of the Wells Tavern. A few years later— perhaps to improve its image—it was rechristened by the newly built church at the top of the hill, which is actually in Hampstead Square. At the corner with Well Road, **Acrise Cottage** has a Kentish name: it was converted from an old stable belonging to the second Spa, with a china cupboard made from a hay-chute. **No. 55** was the last home of popular novelist Pamela Frankau, who died here in 1967. Most of **Nos. 57 and 59**, Christchurch Place, were built by Herbert Marnham as workers' flats, at the same time as their neighbours in Grove Place (q.v.). The northernmost segment is, however, dated 1903. **Christchurch School**, designed in Tudor style by W. and E. Habershon, dates from 1855. Behind here, CHRISTCHURCH PASSAGE follows an old path seen on the 1746 map. It was called West View Lane in the mid nineteenth century, and led to the Ebenezer Strict Baptist Chapel, used by a splinter group from the Holly Mount congregation.

On the other side of Christchurch Hill **No. 26**, long

known as Sunnybank, dates from the early nineteenth century. **Nos. 16–22** display their dates, 1877–78, and a crested K, which means they were built by Charles Bean King of Church Row. The author Ivor Brown and his wife, Irene Hentschel, respected drama critic and drama director respectively, lived at No. 20 for half a century until their recent deaths. She was daughter of Carl Hentschel, the original of Harris in *Three Men in a Boat*.

Off Well Road is CANNON LANE, bristling with late eighteenth-century cannon bollards and early nineteenth-century lamp-posts: they are all listed. Behind the ancient wall on the left, the garden of Cannon Hall has been growing houses, so the door to the old **lock-up** is not what it used to be: it is now the entrance to **No. 11**, complete with answerphone. The Hampstead plaque explains that the lock-up was used from about 1730 to 1830, when business was transferred to Holly Walk. Daphne du Maurier, who grew up in Cannon Hall, described in *Growing Pains* the game she played in this cell, 'its blackened walls and barred slit windows daunting to whichever of us was taking the part of the prisoner at the time'.

At the top of the Hill, SQUIRE'S MOUNT took its name from Joshua Squire, who built the fine residence of that name in 1714. The house has since been divided, one part being called **Chestnut Lodge**, with a neo-Georgian addition by Horace Field. The family of Edwin Field, the law reformer, lived in the main house for many years and left it to the National Trust. Edwin died in 1871, after rescuing a man from the Thames. In the late 1930s this was the home of Clive Brook, star of silent films (remember *Christine of the Hungry Heart*?) and talkies

(remember *Cavalcade*?). The charming terrace of cottages, **Nos. 1–5**, is labelled 'Squires Mount Croft 1704', but this is misleading. The terrace is basically mid-nineteenth-century and the date tablet is thought to have come from a house at the rear, visible on the 1746 map. **No. 12**, one of a pair of new houses with an early Victorian look, was the home around 1960 of Sandy Wilson (see Denning Road).

CANNON PLACE has bigger cannon bollards and the stately **Cannon Hall**, dating from about 1720 but much altered. The cannons and the house name came from Sir James Cosmo Melville, Secretary to the East India Company, who lived at the Hall from 1838. Part of the outbuilding with the cupola was once a magistrates' court, which dealt with the prisoners in the lock-up (see above). Sir Gerald du Maurier, who lived here from 1916 until his death in 1934, used the room for billiards. Sir Gerald (see plaque) was the first Captain Hook in *Peter Pan* (1904) and one of the last great actor-managers. He was son of George du Maurier (q.v.) and father of Daphne. Next door **No. 12**, Cannon Lodge, is mid eighteenth-century, with fish-tail tile-hanging. This was the parsonage of Christ Church before the present vicarage was built as **No. 10**.

The houses on the north side, **Nos. 7–25**, were built in the grounds of old Heathfield House by William Shepherd in 1875–77: they were originally called Heathfield Gardens. In the 1880s the poet W. J. Cory (see Pilgrim's Lane) was living at No. 25 and, at about the same time, the composer, Walford Davies, was using No. 15 as home from home. He was organist at Christ Church in the 1890s and during this time redesigned the organ.

The blue plaque on **No. 5** shows that Sir Flinders Petrie, a pioneer of systematic archaeology, lived here from 1919 to 1935, when not actually digging up Egypt. **No. 1**, which shows its date, 1879, is one of many local studio houses by Batterbury and Huxley.

At the entrance to HAMPSTEAD SQUARE is **Christ Church**, which was built in 1852 by the rich congregation of Well Walk Chapel. The architect was Samuel Dawkes, noted for his railway stations and for Colney Hatch Lunatic Asylum (the centre-piece of Friern Hospital). In the 1860s, the great George Gilbert Scott, living in Admiral's House, became consulting architect and added a west gallery, but this was later removed. In the 1870s his eponymous son supervised repairs to the spire, a great local landmark, and added the west porch. Ewan Christian (see above) designed the north aisle. Records show that on one Sunday in 1886 2,325 people attended this church: the comparable figure in 1902/3 was 909. The coming of Christ Church turned Hampstead Square into a polygon. The 1762 map shows a rectanglular grove here, called The Square: this open space was used in the early nineteenth century by strolling players and later by the Victoria Tea Gardens.

There are several houses of age and beauty here. **No. 1**, which like **No. 2** dates from about 1720, has recently been the home successively of Norman St John Stevas and the Rt Hon. and Rev. The Lord Beaumont. **Nos. 7-9**, a terrace of about 1730, bear a memorial to Newman Hall, a once-famous Congregational minister and hymn-writer, whose widow adapted two houses into homes for the aged. Newman Hall died in 1902 at **No. 6**, an early eighteenth-century house, once called Vine House and still having a vine in view. **No. 11** was the last home of the Rev. John Llewelyn Davies (1826-1916), father of Margaret (see Well Walk) and, like her, a great champion of women's rights. He supported so many unfashionable causes that he was transferred from St Marylebone to distant Kirkby Lonsdale, but he was finally appointed Honorary Chaplain to George V. **No. 12**, Lawn House, is very early eighteenth-century, with flush-framed windows and later extensions. The poet and mystic, Evelyn Underhill, lived here in the 1930s and died here in 1941: she is buried in the parish churchyard. She was a disciple of Baron von Hügel (see Holford Road), a collaborator of Tagore and revered by T. S. Eliot. She has been called a 'very human, very English saint'.

The terrace next door, **Nos. 10-14**, is in ELM ROW and was built in the eighteenth-century over the stables of the Duke of Hamilton in New End: the cottages have recently been refurbished and offered at £80,000 or so each. The grander terrace, **Nos. 1, 3 and 5**, dates from about 1720, but was mostly refaced in the late nineteenth century by local builder C.B. King: the *fleurs de lys* on the front are his marks (c.f. Church Row). No. 3 has a Hampstead plaque to Sir Henry Cole, who lived here in 1879-80. Apart from being largely responsible for founding the Victoria and Albert Museum, where a Henry Cole wing has recently been opened, he is said to have originated the custom of sending Christmas cards. In 1923 D. H. Lawrence stayed some months at No. 1, in the room with the verandah, and used the area as background for his story, *The Last Laugh*. When this house was modernised in the 1970s, it was described by *Good Housekeeping* at the time as 'a rural retreat just a beat away from the pulse of

Hampstead'. Elm Lodge, **No. 2**, was built about 1732 and used to face New End: this may explain its present blank look, with more windows bricked up than glazed. The flights of steps were added about 1930, when the house was split up. There was a row of elms down this street in the eighteenth century.

Round the corner between 114 and 116 Heath Street is the entrance to STAMFORD CLOSE, a nearly secret passage leading to Hampstead Square: it is visible on the 1762 map. In the 1930s, when six old cottages here were condemned, the Close was said to be 'a miserable dark square—a black spot'. Its name derives from nearby Stamford Lodge (now demolished), where in 1823 Constable and his family were among the lodgers.

HOLFORD ROAD takes its name from a worthy Hampstead family of the nineteenth century, involved in the Parish School, the Literary and Scientific Society, the Rifle Volunteers *et al.*: they lived in a mansion round the corner in East Heath Road. The blue plaque on **No. 4** salutes the theologian, Friedrich von Hügel (see above), Baron of the Holy Roman Empire, who lived here from 1882–1903. Among many local good deeds, he helped rescue St Mary's, Holly Place, from closure at the turn of the century. **No. 4b** was the home in the 1960s of Jane Lane, the prolific historical novelist. The towering **High Close** was built by W. H. Murray in 1884 and soon became a guest house, and then a rest house, and is now an old people's home.

At the top of East Heath Road, near Whitestone Pond, is WHITESTONE LANE, which leads to a handsome huddle of houses. Of these **Gangmoor**, which is early eighteenth century, was briefly the home of George du Maurier and family in the 1860s. 'A more genial home', he wrote, 'could not be found anywhere.' **Whitestone House**, once called The Lawn, is of Regency origin, but was much enlarged by Clough Williams Ellis in 1934. Under the lawn were found foundations of a studio, used presumably by the artist, Mark Anthony, who died here in 1886, and possibly by Constable, who rented the adjoining Albion Cottage in 1820. Sir Herbert Barker, the controversial bone-setter or, rather, 'manipulative surgeon', lived at The Lawn from 1912. He was the champion of 'unqualified practitioners', whose gift of healing saved over 30,000 patients from needing operations or appliances. **The Cottage** was rebuilt in 1908 for the widow of Sir Joseph Duveen (see Spaniards Road). In 1933–5 the champion boxer, Jimmy Wilde, lived here and renamed it, for obvious reasons, Lonsdale: he was often seen at the gymnasium at 64 Heath Street. On the pavement nearby is a bewildering **bollard**, marked 'Sommers Town 1817', which has strayed in from another part of London.

Once known as Middle Heath Road, EAST HEATH ROAD was finally so named in the 1860s. A century later it was threatened with plans to turn it into the Hampstead Village By-Pass, but the dreaded six-lane motorway never materialised. At the top of the hill, **Bellmoor** flats are named after the imposing residence on this site of Thomas Barratt, author of the monumental *Annals of Hampstead*, who lived there 1877–1914. Barratt made his money from Pears' Soap, whose image he boosted with the *Bubbles* advertisement and *Pears Cyclopaedia*. Apart from a brown plaque to Barratt, the flats bear a note of their height above sea level (435½ ft) and above the cross of St

Paul's (16½ ft). Among early flat-dwellers here in the 1930s were Bunny Austin, Wimbledon winner, and Sir Thomas Beecham.

No. 22, Ladywell Court, is the remains of a mansion that was the home of the Holford family, commemorated in Holford Road (see their history in *Camden History Review* 6). The house was known as Heathfield in the 1870s, when the grounds were sold for building and the Hampstead Reformatory School for girls moved here from Church Row. Its present healthy name came with its use as a nursing home from before the first World War. The whole building was reconditioned in the 1950s.

Lower down the hill is **No. 17**, which bears an official plaque to the writer Katherine Mansfield and her husband, Middleton Murry. They moved here soon after their marriage in 1918. The house was then called 2 Portland Villas but, as it was tall and grey, they called it The Elephant. In the autumn of 1920, when Hampstead air had failed to cure the writer's consumption, she moved to Italy. **Nos. 14 and 15** are two charming cottages, built in 1770 and traditionally once used by shepherds: the property now belongs to the National Trust. **Foley House** is thought to be the residence built for himself in 1698 by Duffield, the first Spa manager, at the then high cost of a thousand pounds. Apparently named after a Captain Foley, who lived here in 1805–8, the house was leased in the 1880s to Edward Gotto of The Logs: it was he who added the porch and developed part of the grounds. The old stables are included in the DOE Listing.

The block of flats on the north side, **The Pryors**, were allowed on the Heath because there had been a house on this site for many years. This belonged to Thomas Pryor, a rich brewer, who married one of the Hoares of Hampstead in 1802. Before demolition in 1902, the house was occupied by landscape artist, Walter Field, son of Edwin of Squire's Mount: a splendid example of his work is in the Burgh House music room. The flats, designed in Edwardian baroque by Hall and Waterhouse, have accommodated a number of literary gents, notably novelist Ernest Raymond, author of *We, the Accused* and many other absorbing tales. As a change from all the Captain Hooks who populate these pages, the Pryors can boast a famous Peter Pan—Jean Forbes Robertson, who lived here with her actor husband, André van Gyseghem, from the 1930s.

Opposite the flats, **No. 8** was built by Ewan Christian at the same time, and with the same chimneys, as his 50 Well Walk. Controversial philosopher Cyril Joad lived for many years at **No. 4**, which he found 'ugly but comfortable'. Acclaimed for his performances on the BBC's Brains Trust, he also won local fame in the 1930s for championing mixed hockey on the Heath, until then forbidden: he died in 1953 and was buried in the parish churchyard. Kingsley Martin, editor of *The New Statesman*, shared this house with him during the last war.

The creeper-covered **East Heath Lodge** and the semi-detached **South Lodge**, which is in HEATH SIDE, were built about 1820. The former was the home of Sir Arthur Bliss in the 1930s: the latter has its original doorcase with Tower-of-Winds capitals (see Athens, but not in this book). Both have handsome railings with double-axe gateposts. **Nos. 1 and 2** Heathside are a delightful pair of bow-fronted cottages, dating from 1805. The iron balcony pre-dates the houses, as it is said to be by James Wyatt in 1775.

Downshire Hill, 1842, with St Michael's, Highgate, on the skyline. *From a steel engraving by Harwood.*

South End Road, about 1900, showing the Old Engine House. *From a postcard.*

The Late Developers

THE WILLOW ROAD area is shown in a Chatelaine engraving of 1752, and it includes a wide track leading up to the second Long Room in Well Walk. The willows arrived in 1845, when Sir Thomas Maryon Wilson planted a great many trees on the Heath despite—or possibly because of—the protests of his copyholders. The original track ran beside a branch of the Fleet River, which rose under New End School and is still visible there. By 1829, the riverbed in Willow Road had become a popular dumping ground and was described as 'an exposed sewer', which may have discouraged earlier development, but certainly encouraged fine beds of watercress. Most of the present houses in the street are about a hundred years old.

In 1938 the modern terrace, **Nos. 1–3**, replaced an eighteenth-century row of cottages in what the architect, Ernö Goldfinger, called 'an adaptation of eighteenth-century style'. His design brought much protest from local preservationists, but had strong support from architectural pundits. **Nos. 12–14** are an ornate trio showing their date, 1879. In Edwardian times **No. 22** was the home of Roger Fry, pioneer of Post-Impressionism. The attractive **Nos. 33–41**, labelled Willow Cottage's (*sic*), were built about 1866 on the site of some almshouses: traditionally the new cottages were to house watercress pickers. No. 40 achieved fame in the 1970s when its occupants, Lawrence and Pat Hutchins, wrote a story

about it for *Jackanory*: this was *The House that Sailed Away*, which was later published. The old shop front of **No. 49** now shows pottery, instead of the grocery it offered for years: the Russian scholar, David Magarshack, lived above the shop until his recent death.

On the other side of the road, **Willow Hall**, formerly Willow Buildings, began life in 1863 as Militia Barracks (see Burgh House): they were built as married quarters for sergeants and bandsmen, and the design was probably based on Prince Albert's model dwellings, shown at the Great Exhibition in 1851. By 1964 they were in a far from model condition and an eight-year battle began for their improvement. They now belong to Camden Council.

In the middle of the nineteenth century, a large paddock at the north-west end of Willow Road was divided into about forty allotments. By 1870 these had been redeveloped into GAYTON ROAD and CRESCENT. The owner of this four-acre site was barrister George Nathan Best, of Bayfield Hall in Norfolk, and the fact that there is a village called Gayton (meaning goat farm) not far away has suggested this as the origin of the street name. There is also the theory that one of the Potter family, who built the houses here, had Gayton as a second name: but history does not relate which was christened first, the street or the Potter. The whole area was brightened in the 1970s by the formation of the Gayton Residents' Association, aimed at fighting rat runs and pavement parkers and other environmental pests, and responsible for Hampstead's first series of street festivals.

Among distinguished residents in Gayton Crescent in the 1970s were author John Le Carré at **No. 1**, and film director Karel Reisz at **No. 8**. The modern terrace **Nos. 18–22** were built, with others in Gayton Road, on the Gayton Nursery Garden site in 1970. The architects were Ted Levy, Benjamin and Partners, so adept at squeezing attractive pints into half-pint plots. From the first, the no-nonsense houses in Gayton Road attracted a good mix of professional classes and workers, with a preponderance of dressmakers. In the 1880s, **No. 10** was the Hampstead High School for Girls 'under Influential Patronage'. Around 1908, **No. 9** was the home of essayist Robert Lynd and, in the 1970s, of another literary lion, Melvyn Bragg. **No. 61**, the OXFAM shop, has previously been an ironmonger's, a dairy and a betting shop: one of the dairyman's daughters is said to have been Ethel Le Neve, friend of Dr Crippen.

Between Gayton Road and Downshire Hill, the large Carlile House and its grounds were sold to the British Land Company for building in 1875. The resultant streets are full of Victorian middle-class town houses, complete with attics for skivvies. WILLOUGHBY ROAD, which partly followed the drive of Carlile House, was named after the Willoughby family who actually sold the estate. Benjamin Willoughby, a solicitor, had married Edward Carlile's daughter. His second son, incidentally, became Mayor of Holborn and also had a street named after him there. At the High Street end, **Trinity Close** was converted in the 1970s from the hall of the Trinity Presbyterian Church, erected in 1862 (before the road was built) and demolished a century later. The Air Training Corps **hall** next door, with two foundation stones—one saying 'We will do thee good'—was built as a YMCA in 1886.

Another hall opposite, **Rosslyn Hall**, has a longer history. 'A Meeting Place for Protestant Dissenters' was registered in 1691 at Carlile House, then the home of Isaac Honeywood but, when the congregation grew, Honeywood built a chapel next to his stables on this site. This was rebuilt in 1828 and much of Rosslyn Hall's present structure dates from this time. But by 1862 it again proved too small and the present chapel (see Rosslyn Hill) was built nearby; the hall was then used mainly as a school.

No. 14 was the home of Don Salvador de Madariaga in 1916–21: he was a scholarly Anglo-Spanish writer of great style. **No. 26** shows its date (1883) and the initials of its first owner, C. J. Coates. The house clearly pre-dates No. 24, as its side window now has no view whatsoever. Christopher Coates not only ran a China and Glass Warehouse in the High Street, but was Registrar of Marriages and Collector of the Poor Rate. In 1852 his lodger in his High Street house (now demolished) was the struggling artist, Ford Madox Brown. D. H. Lawrence and his wife, Frieda, had rooms at **No. 30**, then called Carlingford House, in the autumn of 1926. Several of his literary circle visited him there and one of them noted 'how depressing and void he found the eighteenth-century charm of Hampstead'. George Orwell was also critical of this area in his *Keep the Aspidistra Flying*, written in the mid 1930s when he was working in a bookshop in South End Green: he immortalised this street as the 'dingy, depressing' Willowbed Road.

RUDALL CRESCENT's name was officially approved in 1877 but, along with several other developments by the British Land Company, its derivation is unknown. The most famous artist to use **Penn Studio** behind No. 13 was Mark Gertler, who came here in 1915 and stayed for seventeen years. From an East End Jewish family, 'by his talents, vivacity and exotic beauty' says the DNB, 'he gained early entry into artistic and intellectual circles'. In this studio he entertained Lytton Strachey, gave tea to Aldous Huxley, found lodgings for D. H. Lawence (see above), and painted the portrait of Sir Arthur Bliss (q.v.). He later used a studio in Well Road, where he has recently been plaqued, and after his marriage in 1930 he lived in KEMPLAY ROAD at **No. 22**. This is another inexplicable street name on the Carlile House estate, though traditionally all the roads were named after friends of Mr Carlile. When the estate was sold up, supporters of Rosslyn Hill Chapel bought up the sites of **Nos. 5–7** and **13–21** to stop the chapel being 'hemmed in by houses of an inferior class'. After many years' use as tennis courts, the derelict land was bought by the Council in 1953 and these houses built. The YWCA, which has just been celebrating its centenary in Hampstead, opened its hostel at **Nos. 6–8** in 1901. Norman del Mar, congenial conductor of many a Promenade Concert, lived at **No. 1a** in the 1950s.

CARLINGFORD ROAD could well be named after Lord Carlingford, who succeeded Peel as Chief Secretary for Ireland and was raised to the peerage in 1874, the year before the road was built. In 1912 another young East End artist, Isaac Rosenberg, who studied at the Slade with Gertler and Stanley Spencer, was living miserably at **No. 32**. His studio-lodging was a bare room, with packing case furniture and broken windows, and by 1914 he earned so little from his art and his poetry that he joined the army: he was killed four years later on the Somme, but his war poems are his lasting glory.

DENNING ROAD was developed from 1878, mainly by local builders Allison and Foskett. From the 1890s, **No. 4** was Miss Slipper's girls' school, but the schoolgirl then at **No. 25** was patronising the North London Collegiate. This was the future family planner, Marie Stopes, living here uneasily with her parents. In particular, she was embarrassed by her archaeological father bringing so many boxes of fossils into the house that the neighbours thought he was a grocer. Ms Stopes has recently been awarded a plaque in Well Walk. A maisonette at **No. 34a** was the home in the 1930s of the Presbyterian family of Sandy Wilson, who wrote that certain thing called *The Boy Friend*. They came to Hampstead, he said, because 'it had been since the 1890s a sort of colony for expatriate Scots, the wealthier of whom built themselves pseudo-baronial mansions'. Note the sunflowers on this and adjoining houses, and the ripe pomegranates on **Nos. 29–33**, with pretty canopies and the date 1880. **No. 38**, long known as Denning Hall, is labelled 'Asked of God, 1883'. It was built as a Mission Hall for St Stephen's but has been converted into artists' studios.

PILGRIM'S LANE takes its name from Charles Pilgrim, who owned land around here and lived in Vane House on Rosslyn Hill. The road was originally a cul-de-sac from Rosslyn Hill as far as the double bend, but around 1880 it was joined to the newer northern stretch, known as Worsley Road. In 1968 the inhabitants of Worsley Road successfully petitioned to be included in Pilgrim's Lane and the whole street was renumbered. Two Worsleys were ministers of St John's, Downshire Hill, the parsonage of which is now **No. 64**. Across the road, next to a Moroccan oasis, **No. 41** was Mark Gertler's lodgings during his Rudall Crescent period. **Nos. 40–44** are on the site of St Stephen's National School, which by 1910 had become the Branch Library until that moved to Keats Grove in 1934. **No. 7** is a late eighteenth-century house, which once had two service wings. Only one has survived: this is now **No. 9**, Cossey Cottage. **Nos. 1 and 3** were built by Horace Field about 1896, along with the bank at the corner.

A plaque on **No. 8** salutes that curious character, W. J. Cory, Eton master ('a brilliant tutor' says the DNB), who left the school mysteriously, assumed a new surname, married a rector's daughter less that half his age, and ended his days in Hampstead teaching classics to young ladies. Best remembered now as the author of the *Eton Boating Song*, he came to Pilgrim's Lane from Cannon Place in 1891 and died here the following year. The courtyard behind the house is decidedly eye-catching. In the 1970s, Daniel Barenboim and Jacqueline du Pré made music at **No. 5a** in their sound-proof studio. In 1982 the great abstract artist, Ben Nicholson, died at **No. 2b**, not far from the Mall Studios off Haverstock Hill, where he had spent 'one of the happiest periods of his life': that was in the 1930s with Barbara Hepworth and their triplets. **No. 2a**, Rosslyn Hill House, is the only house left from an early nineteenth-century row, which stretched to Downshire Hill. The other houses allowed shops to be built on their Rosslyn Hill frontages, and only the shops have survived. The Nevinsons, who were early occupants of Rosslyn Hill House, were a famously benevolent Hampstead family and progenitors of H. W., the Grand Duke of journalism, and his artist son, C. R. W. Nevinson, the apostle of Futurism.

The Downshire Hill triangle, embracing Keats Grove and the upper part of South End Road, is one of the great pleasures of Hampstead. A satisfying number of the stuccoed brick Regency villas have survived, mostly in well-kept terraces with rich gardens in front. Nearly all of them have stayed family houses, avoiding relegation into flats and lodgings, and most are listed buildings, as a 'group of considerable merit'. In its early days, the area was known as the Lower Heath quarter, or sometimes as the Brickfield. Apart from this industry, there is some evidence of cottages and farm buildings existing here on the edge of the Heath before the developers arrived.

DOWNSHIRE HILL was a dignified development of the early nineteenth century. Its exact date of birth is not recorded, but it must have been just before 1814, when the southern part appears on Park's map of Hampstead. The street name, first seen in the 1819 Rate Books, perhaps relates to the first Marquis of Downshire, with the apt family name of Hill, who achieved some fame as Secretary of State for the colonies and, in particular, for his harsh policy towards America.

At the south-west end, **No. 1b**, dated 1891 on its front, started as a postal sorting office, became a Social Security office, and is now a puppet studio. The original villas begin with **Nos. 4–6**, all bow-fronted and balconied, and continue with **Nos. 7–8**, all Gothic and crenellated. The poet, Edwin Muir, lived at No. 7 in the early 1930s and described its plumbing and other problems in his autobiography; but he forgave the house its troubles as he was 'in love with its sweet, battered, Mozartian grace'. In the late thirties, this was the home of tennis champion, Bunny Austin. At the turn of the century Gordon Craig, the revolutionary stage designer, shared rooms in No. 8 with composer Martin Shaw. Though already married, Craig eloped with Elena Meo, the daughter of an artist who lived across the road at No. 39 (q.v.). The latter was reconciled to his daughter only by the intervention of Craig's mother, the great Ellen Terry, who regarded Elena as her 'favourite daughter-in-law'. The poet, Sylvia Lynd (née Dryhurst) was born at **No. 11** in 1887: one of her poems described the house's wonderful wistaria. After her marriage to Robert Lynd, they moved to **No. 14** until 1918 and later to Keats Grove.

No. 14a introduces a sudden classical note into this Georgian row—perhaps because it was built as a temple of learning for the St John's Chapel School. Founded by the minister, the Rev. John Wilcox, in the early 1830s, the school grew rapidly and by 1846 accommodated ninety-six boys and sixty girls. By 1885 it had become St Stephen's National School, which was later extended into Pilgrim's Lane (q.v.). The 'temple' took on a new lease of life during the first World War as the studios of the Carline family. Based at No. 47, they were not only artists themselves, but attracted a large circle of modern painters, variously known as the Hampstead Set or the Downshire Hill Group. Hilda Carline became Stanley Spencer's first wife and he, together with Henry Lamb,

Mark Gertler, C. R. W. Nevinson, Robert Bevan and many others, would meet here and at No. 47 to paint and talk and, at least once, throw a fancy dress party for two hundred people. The place seemed to appeal to artists, as Richard Carline said 'especially at mealtimes'.

Nos. 16–17 are labelled Portland Place and dated 1823, while **Nos. 18–19** have an illegible name plaque, which once said Weymouth Place. Before the last war, **No. 21** was the home of art expert Sir Roland Penrose, and after the war of John Bainbridge, the versatile Australian artist. Between **Nos. 23 and 24** is the entrance to what was the Hampstead Heath Riding School and, before that, livery stables. In 1873 Walter Hill, son of the local publican, is shown as a cab proprietor here and in 1885 his brother, William is licensed to hire dog carts and tricycles. The horses moved out in 1962.

In their early days, **Nos. 25–26** were known as Langham Place, and the former was briefly the home of John Constable and his family. The artist was already in the habit of coming to Hampstead for the summer at least, and had rented four different local houses, notably one in Lower Terrace, before choosing Downshire Hill in 1826. Writing to his friend, C. R. Leslie, in December that year he says: 'We are in No. 1 Langham Place, Downshire Hill, a spot in a valley just before you enter the town. Our house is to the left of the new chapple (*sic*).'

No. 31 figures in the Vestry Minutes of 1873 because it overlooked Tibbles' Yard and the householder complained about the pigs and refuse. 'The smell is very bad,' he wrote, 'and the lodgers won't stop.' But there were no complaints from **The Freemasons' Arms**, which is first mentioned in the Rate Books of 1819. Frequently rebuilt and extended to cater for modern tastes and thirsts, the latest main revision was in 1936 and involved battles with the River Fleet, which flows underneath. The pub was until recently famous for its Pell Mell court. It was originally a Flemish game imported by Charles II after his exile and introduced in Pall Mall, which soon took the name of the game. Played in the open, the game involved heavy balls held by rings at the ends of poles and thrown through round hoops on a swivel.

Across the road are further cottages of the early and mid nineteenth century variety. Professor J. D. Bernal, physicist and philosopher of science, lived at **No. 35** in the late 1930s: among his many achievements was the design of the Mulberry Harbours for the last war's D-Day. **No. 36** was Sir Roland Penrose's post-war home, and **No. 37** Flora Robson's pre-war prestigious address. After her success as Elizabeth I in *Fire over England* in 1936, she was put under contract by Alexander Korda, which allowed her to take 'a smart house in Downshire Hill, buy a car and engage a chauffeur'. Tony Greenwood, Baron Greenwood of Rossendale, who lived at **No. 38** until his recent death , was *inter alia* Labour's Minister of Housing in the late 1960s. During his cabinet days, he had an office built in the garden with his own scrambler phone link to No. 10 Downing Street. **Nos. 39 and 40** and the terraced **Nos. 41–43** were all built in 1825 and by 1849 were owned by the Duke of Devonshire. Nos. 39 and 41 were at various times the home of Italian artist Gaetano Meo and his large family, one of whom fell in love with the occupant of No. 8. Meo began as the much-loved model of Samuel Butler, Rossetti and other Pre-Raphaelites, notably Henry Holiday, who made him his assistant at his Redington Gardens studio. Meo's poor English was occasionally a problem, as he captioned a Holiday cartoon of Moses in the bullrushes as Moses in the Bull and Bush. Meo died at No. 41 in 1925 but his daughter, Taormina, owned the house until 1957. The author and advocate of women's rights, Amber Blanco White, who died recently at **No. 44**, was a close friend of H. G. Wells (see 17 Church Row) and bore him a daughter: he modelled his *Ann Veronica* on her New Woman.

The centrepiece of this area is the splendidly situated, and recently re-roofed, **St John's Church**. Most local histories say that the building dates from 1818, but the present church was definitely not opened to public worship until 1823. The church guide suggests that its builder, William Woods from Kennington, was also its designer. Woods, who developed much of the Downshire Hill area, using quantities of local bricks from old farm buildings and brickfields, built a very similar chapel in North Brixton. The church, with its elegant portico and cupola, galleries and box pews, is a delight both outside and in. Like the old Well Walk chapel, it was probably intended as a chapel-of-ease to Hampstead Parish Church, also dedicated to St John, but it became a proprietary chapel (that is, privately owned), and is now the last of its kind in London.

Among Downshire Hill's many artistic associations, **No. 47** was the home of the Carline family (see No. 14a), who lived here from 1914–36. Richard Carline (1896-1980) was prime mover of the Hampstead Artists Council, founded in 1944, and became UNESCO's first art consultant in 1945: he appears as a reviving corpse in Stanley Spencer's *A Cookham Resurrection*, painted in the

Vale of Health. Just before the last war, No. 47 became the headquarters of the Artists' Refugee Committee under Stephen Bone. One refugee, who was invited to lodge here for two weeks and stayed for five years, was the German Dadaist, John Heartfield, credited with the invention of photo-montage.

The ground drops away behind **No. 49**, which has its entry at first floor level, and this may have prompted the baseless belief that the house was a hunting lodge that pre-dates the street. The poet, Anna Wickham, one of D. H. Lawence's circle, lived here early this century and wrote a poem about the house. In the 1960s this was the home of architect and town-planner, Sir Frederick Gibberd, responsible for such epics as London Airport and Harlow New Town. The glass box at **No. 49a** caused some local apoplexy when it was built by Michael Hopkins in 1978, but it received a Civic Trust Award the following year and was praised for its 'refreshing clarity and panache'.

Next door is one of the first blocks of flats in the area, **Hampstead Hill Mansions**, showing its building date, 1896. On this site was Spring Cottage, where Rossetti spent a short time in lodgings with Lizzie Siddal, soon after their marriage in 1860. Lizzie already liked Hampstead as she had convalesced here after posing for long hours in the bathtub for Millais's *Ophelia*. Rossetti, on the other hand, had said that Hampstead was 'pretty well beyond civilisation'. After a mainly Regency ramble, this tour of Downshire Hill finishes on a sober twentieth-century note with **Hampstead Magistrates' Court**, built in 1934 as a convenient appendage to the Police Station in Rosslyn Hill.

KEATS GROVE has also kept many of its Regency villas and cottages intact. Much of the north side dates from about 1820, as Keats himself confirmed in a letter that year from Wentworth Place: 'The half-built houses opposite . . . seem dying from old age before they are bought up.' The first name for the street was Albion Grove, seen on the 1829 map, but soon after it became John Street, probably in reverence to St John's Church. It was not until 1910 that the road was named after its most famous resident. Orwell called it Coleridge Grove in *Keep the Aspidistra Flying*.

No. 1, with an attractive Gothic porch, was until recently the home of Marjorie Rackstraw (1888–1981), founder of Hampstead Old People's Housing Trust: a block of flats in Primrose Hill Road is named after her. In the 1930s **Nos. 4a and 5** were peppered with poets and critics—Louis MacNeice and Geoffrey Grigson at the former, and Robert and Sylvia Lynd at the latter, and Edwin Muir was just up the road. Grigson founded and edited his magazine *New Verse* here, and called one of his prose poems *Uccello on the Heath*.

No doubt all these poets were inspired by the proximity of **Keats House**. Originally known as Wentworth Place, it was built in 1815–16, one of the first houses in the street. It was a joint venture by the antiquary and critic, Charles Wentworth Dilke, and his friend, Charles Armitage Brown, and the design ingeniously disguised the fact that it was really a semi-detached or duplex villa, with two front doors. The Dilke family used the central one, and Brown had his entrance round the side. Keats moved in with Brown in 1818 after his brother, Tom, had died at their noisy lodgings in Well Walk.

About this time he met Fanny Brawne and in the spring

of 1819, on Dilke's departure, her family took over his part of Wentworth Place. In May that year, sitting here under a plum tree, Keats wrote his ode to the nightingale that had built its nest in the garden. At the age of twenty-three, this was his summer of supreme poetic achievement: the rest of his story is tragedy. Consumed with tuberculosis, he left Hampstead in 1820 and died in Rome the following year. The Brawne family stayed in Wentworth Place until 1829.

Ten years later, the house was bought by Eliza Chester, a retired actress, who had also held the curious post of Reader to George IV. She converted the property into a single residence and added the new wing. The name was then changed to Lawn Cottage, and later to Lawn Bank. In 1896 the brown plaque to Keats was erected by the Royal Society of Arts, and in 1920–21 the house was rescued from demolition by public subscriptions, largely from America. (Somebody worked out that John Keats was an anagram of Thanks, Joe!) Its future was then vested in the local Council, and from 1925 it was opened to the public. The tall trees along the road fence were probably planted when the house was built, and the mulberry tree is said to date from Stuart times. The garden has recently been replanted in a Regency style suggested by the Garden History Society (hydrangeas, etc.—out, honeysuckle, etc.—in). A plaque records the position of the historic plum tree, which has long since gone, as have the nightingales.

Adjoining Keats House is the **Heath Branch Library**, designed by Sydney Trent, and opened in 1931, together with the Keats Memorial Library, opened by appointment only. Down the road two bollards marked St PPM have wandered in from St Pancras and should be ignored. **No. 12** is a 'spacious, white-walled early nineteenth-century house', says Roy Jenkins, in his biography of H. H. Asquith. The future Prime Minster came here in 1877, after his first marriage, and here ten years later his only daughter was born, the future Lady Violet Bonham-Carter. The same year the family moved to the 'larger, less attractive' 27 Maresfield Gardens, where a plaque has now been erected.

Nos. 19–22 are charming cottages, reputedly built by and for workers in the local brickfield. Dame Edith Sitwell lived briefly and died calmly at No. 20 in 1964. To an enquirer after her health, she is said to have replied: 'I am dying, but otherwise quite well.' She renamed the cottage Bryher House after the novelist of that name who was her friend and patron. **No. 24** displays a large Ancient Lights sign on its side wall to warn off any building that comes too near.

Two houses on the other side of the road were demolished in 1900 to make way for HEATH HURST ROAD. The road was originally called Heathurst, but was changed in 1902—perhaps because the residents objected to a slur on their name? **No. 7** was the home for many years of the remarkable artist, Gerald Ososki, the son of an East End Jewish tailor. Apart from his own painting, he launched a decorating and restoration business, whose contracts included the Houses of Parliament and the State Ballroom at Buckingham Palace. One of his Hampstead Heath views can be seen at Burgh House.

At the corner with SOUTH END ROAD is the oldest **bakery** in North London, bearing an 1897 plaque and the initials of its founder, William Rumbold. For many years it was a bakery-cum-post office. In a northerly direction (as the southern stretch belongs to another book), the terrace of **shops** was built in 1898 and called Station Parade. **Nos. 71 and 73** are an impressive Regency pair, the former (Russell House) having alterations by Charles Voysey in 1890—his earliest surviving work, said Pevsner. The **grove** of trees opposite was planted in the early 1890s over the lowest of the Heath ponds, which had become a public nuisance and was filled in. Between it and the next pond, the Hampstead Water Company sank a deep well in 1835 and installed a steam pumping engine, which they housed in an octagonal tower. This attractive pepperpot, seen in many old prints of the area, later became a residence, but was demolished in 1907 owing to settlement.

The **cottages** across the road are nearly all Regency, but some were badly bombed during the last war and much rebuilt. **No. 79** was the home of Annie Miller, the slum girl whom Holman Hunt groomed as a model and a prospective wife. But when she came here in 1867, she was Mrs Thomas Thompson instead. In 1882, Alfred Harmsworth, later 'the Napoleon of the Press', found digs at **No. 99**. Studies of nineteenth-century censuses, published in *Camden History Review 7*, showed that this street, known as Lower Heath, had a strong working-class element: this applied in fact to the whole Downshire Hill triangle, which did not begin gentrification until the 1920s. It is perhaps significant that **No. 103** was a gardener's cottage from the 1890s to the 1920s, and then became the home of architect Oswald Milne, Alderman and Mayor of Hampstead in 1947–49.

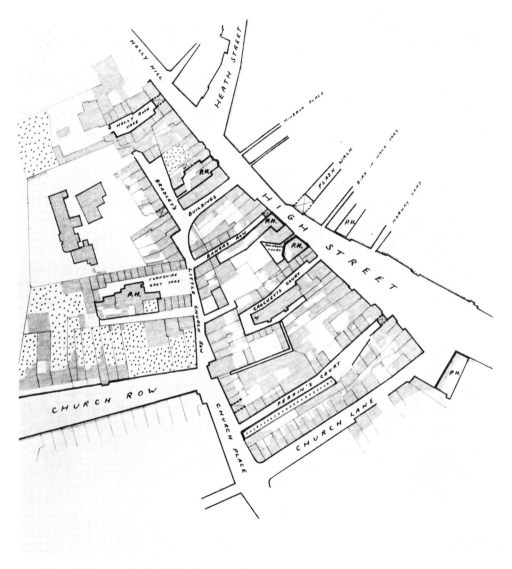

The area between Church Row and the High Street before the Town Improvements of 1887. *Specially drawn by Shirley Harris.*

The Main Roads

TWO main roads climb up to the centre of Hampstead. The Fitzjohns Avenue and lower Heath Street approach is a late nineteenth-century development, but Rosslyn Hill and the High Street follow a very ancient track. The two routes converge on the twisty upper part of HEATH STREET, which makes it one of the most lead-polluted streets in the area. Despite this, it is dotted with boutiques, pubs and eating houses. The street name does not appear in the Rate Books until 1831: the northern end was previously called Heath Mount and the rest was included in the High Street.

On the east side, above the Tube Station (see High Street), is **Kingswell**, announced as 'a new shopping concept by Petty Heath Development Ltd'. The precinct was opened in 1972 to designs by Ted Levy, Benjamin and Partners; the aluminium sculpture is by Robert Adams. The King's Well was the name of the ancient village well near here. In 1312 Robert de Kyngeswell is recorded as a free tenant of the Hampstead manor, who was none-theless obliged to provide the lord annually with two geese and a fowl.

No. 64 at the corner of Back Lane, for many years a restaurant, was opened in 1900 as the Heath Street Club and Gymnasium. From about 1910 it was also the first cinema in the area, variously known as The Eldorado and the Hampstead Picture Palace. By 1916 it had started its catering career as the Tube Tea Rooms. **The Horse and Groom** is mentioned in records of 1840, but has been given a newer, flamboyant facade. The pub should be listed like its neighbours, **Nos. 70–84**, which are all late eighteenth-century or early nineteenth-century. A hundred years ago, **No. 76** housed two cow-keepers, and **No. 82** was the Ancient Smithy, offering non-chic harness, animal medicines and sanitary engineering.

The **Baptist Church**, designed by C. G. Searle, was opened in 1861 and used by many of the congregation established in the Holly Mount chapel. Much of the £6,000 or so needed for the building was supplied by a grateful merchant, who had come to lodge in Heath Street in the hope that Hampstead air would cure his sick son, which it did. The site was part of Campbell's Nursery Garden, which stretched to Mansfield Place and also provided land for the mid nineteenth-century **Nos. 86–90**, still labelled Claremont Terrace. **Nos. 92 and 94** are eighteenth-century and among the oldest survivals in the street. **Nos. 96 and 98**, which are late Georgian, were successively the addresses of E. Arnot Robertson, the novelist and critic: she died in 1961 at No. 98. Called Guyon House after an old Hampstead family, this was also the home from 1937 of Theodore Besterman, founder of the Guyon House Press, which produced fine books, and authority on Voltaire (see 6 The Mount, opposite).

Nos. 112–114 are eighteenth-century, but are better viewed from behind in Stamford Close. **No. 118** is an early nineteenth-century building, which was later known as Mansfield Cottage and occupied by a gardener. From 1879–87, his hermit-like lodger was Henry Sweet, author of *A History of Language*, and described by the DNB as the 'greatest British philologist and chief founder of modern phonetics': among other claims to fame, he was the original of Professor Higgins in *Pygmalion*. The **Friends' Meeting House** next door was designed in 1907 by Fred Rowntree, later responsible for the Quaker village at Jordans in Buckinghamshire. Note the 1836 Hampstead **bollard** at the entrance to Hampstead Square.

Many local parents still call **No. 124** Queen Mary's Maternity Home, but it is now a training centre for the Royal Free Hospital. The previous building here dated back to the early eighteenth-century Spa period, and was known as the Upper Flask Tavern. Here met the distinguished Whig literary and social circle, the Kit Cat Club, including Pope, Addison and Steele, whose portraits by Kneller (he painted every club member) are prominent in the National Portrait Gallery. This tavern also featured in Richardson's novel, *Clarissa*, published in 1748. The building became a private residence soon afterwards, and was variously called Upper Bowling Green House, or just Upper Heath. Here lived George Steevens, co-editor with Samuel Johnson of Shakespeare's works. Lord Leverhulme (see The Hill) gave the site and Queen Mary laid the foundation stone for the model maternity home, built in 1922 with money left over from the royal comforts-for-the-troops fund of the Great War. Her Majesty took a personal interest in

the home, crocheting cot covers and getting her Needlework Guilds to supply all the necessary nighties. Special layettes came from the Montreal Guild for all girls born on the Queen's birthday, who were expected to be called Mary.

Across the street, behind an old wall, was the site of Heath Mount School, which originated in 1817 'for the sons of gentlemen'. Evelyn Waugh was a pupil here in 1911–16, as his diaries record (see also Langland Gardens), and J. S. Granville Grenfell, his headmaster, is supposed to be the model of the head in *Decline and Fall*. The building was demolished in 1934 but the school lives on in Hertfordshire.

Nos. 115–125 make an attractive terrace, dated by the DOE as early nineteenth-century, but some say older. No. 117 has half a millstone on its steps, which may well be a souvenir of the Hampstead windmills. The **Coach and Horses** has been here since Georgian times but, like all pubs, has been much rebuilt. The lovely, late eighteenth-century **Conduit House**, No. 93, was in the greengrocery business in the 1850s, when Ford Madox Brown was painting *Work* (see The Mount): the greengrocery is clearly visible in the background of the picture. **Nos. 83–89** are DOE-dated as early nineteenth-century, but No. 89 has one door inexplicably marked 'Kit Cat House 1745'. **Nos. 69–81** also appear in the DOE lists, all nineteenth-century except No. 75, which is mid-eighteenth: most of the shop fronts have been modernised. The Nag's Head, with its decorated upper storeys, is officially listed 'for curiosity value'. After all these modest period premises, the building at **Nos. 57–61** comes as a shock. It was designed by Peter Clapp for

Drazin's television shop in 1970 and has been praised by the pundits for having 'guts and good manners'.

The Gothic **No. 49**, with the popular clock tower, was built for a fire station by the Metropolitan Board of Works (forerunner of the GLC) in 1873, as various plaques and initials confirm. The tower was also a water tower and this was one of the first buildings for London's new horse-drawn fire brigade to have one. Originally taller than it is now, the tower was a useful observation post in two world wars, though a warning rocket fired in the first war unfortunately did some damage to the nearby Parochial School. The station was closed in 1915 when the new one was opened in Lancaster Grove.

The lower part of Heath Street was almost entirely rebuilt, along with parts of the High Street, in 1887–89, mainly to connect the new Fitzjohns Avenue with upper Heath Street and the High Street. Previously the way through from the south had consisted of narrow, winding and sloping courts and alleys (see plan) and the area had degenerated into slums. The Hampstead Town Improvements were authorised by the Metropolitan Street Improvements Act, passed in 1883, and the new roads were opened to the public in May 1887, at an overall cost of £137,813. The costs were shared by the Hampstead Vestry and the Board of Works, which explains the present ownership of so many houses in this street by Camden Council and the GLC.

Among the new buildings, the grand **Nos. 23–27**, designed by Keith Young, were built for Express Dairies in 1889. (The dairies have recently disappeared, along with nearby Sainsbury's and Boots and other much-loved chains.) **Nos. 15–21** also have an elaborate terra cotta facade, with the date 1888 and initials GP—presumably for land-owner Major George Paget. **No. 13a** provided a studio for (Sir) David Low, the New Zealand-born cartoonist, in the 1930s: then with the *Evening Standard*, he achieved fame by holding *all* political parties up to ridicule with such timeless characters as Colonel Blimp and the TUC carthorse.

Across the road, **No 24** was built by Spalding and Cross for the Hampstead Liberal Club in 1889 (see foundation stone). **The Three Horshoes** was the name of an unlucky pub at 62 High Street, which was displaced during the Town Improvements and rebuilt here.

A number of offshoots from lower Heath Street are worth exploring. At the north-west end, HOLLY BUSH VALE follows the line of a pre-Improvements alley, which was linked up with a court of this name off Holly Hill about 1887. The alley was part of Bradley's Buildings, but was entirely rebuilt. The Wells and Campden Charity erected a tenement block to accommodate some of the displaced persons on the site of **New Campden Court**, which now belongs to Camden. (Those confused by Campden and Camden should reread the Historical Note.)

The **Everyman** Cinema began life in 1888 as a Drill Hall for the Hampstead Rifle Volunteers. In 1919 the windows were blocked up (but some are still visible) for Norman MacDermott's Everyman Theatre, which became one of London's leading Little Theatres. Among other premières, Noel Coward starred here in the first production of his controversial play, *The Vortex*. In 1933 the cinema took over, run for the first forty years by James Fairfax-Jones: it has been called the 'most famous

Church Row, 1886, showing Oriel House and the site of Gardnor Mansions. *From a water-colour by Harold Lawes.*

little cinema in the world'.

Through the archway next door is the Hampstead **Parochial School**, the main buildings dating from 1856–62, but the institution deriving from the 1780s (see history by E. V. Knox). The Moreland Hall was designed in 1893 by Norman Shaw, but much extended in 1938 by Ashley and Newman: it was then named after Richard Moreland, a great benefactor of the Parish Church. The Hampstead Theatre Club, now thriving at Swiss Cottage, began in this hall in 1959. They had success with Pinter premières but problems with, in the director's own words, 'the atmosphere of stale cabbage, carbolic soap and Scouts overhead'.

YORKSHIRE GREY PLACE was named in 1974 (with the help of Camden History Society) after an old inn demolished here in the 1880s. PERRIN'S WALK commemorates the Perrin family, who owned property in this area in the early eighteenth century, including a pub called The Goose. Until 1936, this was called Church Walk, originally consisting of coach houses for Church Row residents: the house numbers still correspond. Thus **No. 24** belonged to 24 Church Row and when the artist, Norman Evill, lived at the latter between the wars, he put his initials on the Perrin's Walk frontage and a Strawberry Hill Gothic facade on the rear. The picturesque **No. 20** was used by Henry Holiday (see Redington Gardens) as his glass works: the kiln chimney is still there. The versatile writer, Eleanor Farjeon, lived here from 1920 until her death in 1965. She is happily remembered for her children's books and the lyric of *Morning has Broken*.

PERRIN'S LANE was also named in 1936, after many years as Church Lane. This was the main route to the church from the High Street, where No. 28 was the parsonage until the 1870s. The south side of this lane has been redeveloped, but **No. 8** is basically mid eighteenth-century and **No. 12** mid nineteenth-century: their shopfronts have been converted to domesticity. **Nos. 14–26** are an attractive early nineteenth-century terrace, and two contemporary gun-bollards, dated 1828, have miraculously survived all the local upheavals. To the south, PRINCE ARTHUR MEWS is first seen in the Rate Books of 1885, but the original buildings are now hardly visible at all. **Prince Arthur Court** is an exception, but these Model Buildings for Workers have recently been gentrified. The name of the mews recalls the opening of Monro House (see Fitzjohns Avenue) by Prince Arthur in 1869.

Back in Heath Street, the next sideshoot is PERRIN'S COURT, which was much altered at the west end during the Town Improvements. The **Village Mount** flats were built then and called Greenhill Flats: they were rebuilt and renamed after a fire in 1975. The **offices** of the *Hampstead and Highgate Express* are on the site of a building that was used successively as a Temperance Hall, a Presbyterian Chapel, a Drill Hall for the Hampstead Volunteers, Salvation Army Headquarters, a cabinet maker's and the Parish Church Institute. The *Ham and High* was first printed in Holly Mount in 1860, but was up for sale within a year. George Jealous bought it and became the first of only four editors since then and now, one of whom was his nephew, Walter. The offices were moved to the High Street in 1883 and to Perrin's Court in 1938, where they were rebuilt around 1960 as a centenary celebration (architect: Mayer Hillman). The paper has since been acquired by Home Counties Newspapers of Luton.

Several old houses have survived at the High Street end, including **Nos. 2–6**, which are early eighteenth-century. Nos. 2 and 4 still have their shopfronts, but have been domesticated. No. 6 has a small original doorway and a large imported Georgian one. **Nos. 1 and 3** were for many years the homes of two famous Hampstead characters. In the former was Bert Matthews, for forty years rat catcher (with dogs and ferrets) to Hampstead Borough Council and, with his wife Rebecca, Pearly King and Queen of Hampstead. In No. 3 lived the last local chimney sweep, Henry Kippin, born here in 1882 to a family of sweeps and carpet beaters: his handcart is preserved at the Hampstead Museum, Burgh House. A covered entrance to the north side leads to the Hampstead **Antique Emporium**, premises previously used by the White Bear Garage and, before that, by Roff and Son, the builders.

The next alley northwards, which was another builders' yard, was called ORIEL COURT after the nearby Oriel House. This building, with a fine orielled bay, was used for mass by the local Roman Catholic congregation before they built St Mary's, Holly Place. The house was swept away by the Improvements, along with the adjoining slum, Crockett's Court, over which was built ORIEL PLACE. Most of the slum dwellers were rehoused in Wells Buildings, erected in 1876 by the Wells Charity Trust (see date and initials). These were renamed **Wells Court** when 'buildings' became a dirty word. The new buildings were very much admired. In 1889 there occurred a minor outbreak of scarlet fever in Hampstead

and a report made to the Vestry at that time stated that, although the buildings contained eighty-six children, the fever was confined to eight cases and did not spread. This success was attributed to the 'excellent sanitary arrangements of these buildings, together with the attention paid to ventilation and the free circulation of air occasioned by the staircases and passages being open to the air'. The tenants were not so happy about these windswept passages and 'grim-looking sub-standard' blocks in the 1960s, until Camden Council took them over and modernised them.

Leading back to Heath Street, the narrow BAKER'S PASSAGE commemorates an old Baker's Row near here. According to Mary Hill, this latter was so called because 'Mr Baker the Curate once rode his horse down it', though the claims of Mr Burck the baker, at 59 High Street in the 1850s, seem more relevant.

In the fifteenth century HAMPSTEAD HIGH STREET was called Kingswell Street (see above), and in later years Hampstead Street and Hampstead Hill. These three names have included at times not only the present High Street, but also some or all of the upper part of Heath Street. Other names for parts of it were The Road and The Town because, from the eighteenth century until comparatively recently, Hampstead was 'town' not 'village'. Until the Town Improvements of 1887, the High Street narrowed just above Perrin's Court to become the same width as Holly Hill. The first Improvement idea was to widen the street by demolishing the eastern side, but when the plans were submitted to the Metropolitan Board of Works a deputation of householders protested that this would make them homeless. As the western side concealed decaying property, which the Vestry wished to clear away, it was then decided to remove all the buildings on that side above No. 72: these had their frontages just about in the middle of the present roadway. Many courts and alleys disappeared at the same time.

A cul-de-sac called Minerva Place survived this redevelopment, but later gave way to the Hampstead **Tube Station** (architect: Leslie Green) in 1907. In that year, the line from Charing Cross to Golders Green was opened by Lloyd George. The Hampstead platforms are the deepest in London (192 feet below ground) and became popular air-raid shelters in two world wars. **Nos. 45 and 46**, which are eighteenth-century at the back and terribly twentieth-century at the front, were respectively famous for their drapery (see Mrs Siddons) and grocery businesses for over a century.

Both Flask Walk (q.v.) and BIRD IN HAND YARD had covered entrances and the latter was particularly dangerous for drivers of the London Omnibus Company. In Victorian times, four-horse omnibuses ran regularly from here to the City and Charing Cross, roughly following the present tube routes of the City and Charing Cross lines. The horses were stabled in this yard (now much curtailed) from the 1830s, and at least one drunken bus driver was nearly decapitated for failing to duck at the entrance. The alley was named after a pub at **No. 39**, which was rebuilt in 1879 but has recently become a French café. The bird-in-hand carving remains partly visible, as do the outlines of the old oil jars on **No. 40**. This shop was an oil and colourman's in the 1850s and continued as an ironmonger's until 1979. Fortunately, its two historic oil-jar shop-signs were then rescued for the Hampstead Museum.

On the opposite side, the stationers at **No. 57** are among the few firms which have traded in the High Street for over a hundred years. In the mid 1930s, over the millinery showrooms of Gaze and Co. at **No. 61**, lived and worked the artist, Charles Ginner. A founder-member of Sickert's Camden Town Group, he painted several views down Flask Walk, including a joyous Coronation Day scene in 1937, which is at the Tate. Gaze's, the last of the local drapers, also traded for many years at **Nos. 65 and 66**, and their hallowed name can still be seen writ large on the wall of the former. The supermarket at **Nos. 68–69** is a much disputed site, but the opposition to Woolworths' successful plan for a store here in the 1930s was nothing to the anti-burger battle of fifty years later. The local residents' protests at changing a useful shop into yet another fast food parlour were eventually endorsed by the Environment Secretary. Below here are the older houses, such as **Nos. 70–72**, which are all early eighteenth-century. The first two have kept their Victorian shop fronts. The covered entrance to Perrin's Court, much recorded by local artists, belongs to **No. 73**, which was in the grocery business for over two centuries. This and **Nos. 74–76** are all of eighteenth-century origin.

The William IV became the name of the old King's Head pub after that monarch passed through Hampstead in 1835 on his way to a strawberry feast at Ken Wood: his queen achieved an Adelaide Tavern and Road at the foot of the hill. Next door, the Hampstead **Community Centre** site was first used for the pub's stables, and later for coach builders and motor engineers. This early Victorian building was derelict in the 1970s, when the local Council bought it for a branch library, a plan which is still on the shelf. Since 1976 they have leased it to Hampstead Community Action Ltd for a market and meeting place, the former helping to pay for the latter. The new **post office** also arrived in the 1970s, designed by J. E. Jolly, taking over a site much used by motor showrooms and, from 1883–1938, the offices of the *Ham and High*. The post office was due to be opened in spring 1974 by the Tory Minister of Communications, but on that very day Edward Heath lost the election. **Nos. 83 and 84** are an early eighteenth-century pair, but their roofs are oddly different. At the corner with Prince Arthur Road, **Nos. 85–88** include Stanfield House, built about 1730, which commemorates the artist, Clarkson Stanfield. He lived here from 1847–65 (see plaque). Apart from his seascapes, which earned him the title of the English Van de Velde, he designed stage scenery, notably for amateur productions by his friend, Charles Dickens: a sample is preserved at Dickens House Museum. Many of his large family were baptised at St Mary's, Holly Place, where still hangs his portrait of Abbé Morel. Stanfield was driven away by the development of Prince Arthur Road and died in Belsize Park Gardens. The house, with a hall (by Horace Field) and other additions, was later used *inter alia* for a hospital, a school, the Hampstead Subscription Library and a Christian Science church. It is now divided into four dwellings.

PRINCE ARTHUR ROAD was partly so named in 1872, three years after the prince opened Monro House (q.v.). The western stretch was inexplicably called Lingard Road until 1883. The 1930s blocks of **Greenhill** are on the site of a long-lived mansion called The Rookery, or Mount Grove, which was the home, until 1842, of two successive Longmans, the publishers. The house and the Greenhill estate, which was then owned by Sir John Key, a wholesale stationer and twice Lord Mayor of London, was sold by his son in 1871. A short-lived Wesleyan chapel then stood on the Rookery site until 1935, when the flats began to rise. Dame Edith Sitwell lived for three years at Flat 42, Greenhill, moving in 1964 to Keats Grove, where she died.

Back onto the north side of the High Street, and into the twentieth century, SPENCER WALK is a new luxury development by the Spencer Group to designs by Ian Fraser/John Roberts. The site was also a battlefield in the 1930s, when the ancient Norway House here was demolished to make way for motor engineers, later the Blue Star Garage. **Nos. 30 and 31** High Street are eighteenth-century, but the latter has a late nineteenth-century shop front. **No. 29** has been a chemist's for over a hundred and fifty years, and under the same name for over a hundred. Rebuilt after a fire, the building displays its date (1870) in a riot of romanesque arches. The bank next door, **No. 28**, occupies the old parsonage, probably on the site of an even older parsonage, first mentioned in 1660 according to Barratt. The present building dates from early last century, with a baroque facade added later in the century, when the man of God gave way to Mammon. **No. 27** is mainly eighteenth-century, and the family firm of jewellers has been there since the 1890s. The foot-scraper and the inner door with pince-nez fanlight are worth noting, as is the Austrian dog-clock in the window, which has been putting out its tongue at passers-by since the family opened its first shop in Heath Street in

1891. The Penfold-type **pillar box** near Gayton Road (but liable to be resited) is over a hundred years old and no longer used, but it is preserved as an historic monument.

Below **Nos. 18 and 19**, an early eighteenth-century pair, is MARTY'S YARD, designed by Ted Levy in 1983: he called it 'a bit of an odd-ball development' and named it after the comedian, the late Marty Feldman, who had planned to live here. This alley was the entrance to the abbatoir behind **No. 17**, which for over a century and a half was a butcher's. The Old Bank House, **No. 14** High Street, dates back to the mid-seventeenth century and was part of the Three Tuns Tavern in the eighteenth. This property then belonged to Hampstead's brewer, Robert Vincent, who also owned **The King of Bohemia**. The present pub was built in 1935, but the name is first mentioned in 1680. Though the inn sign now favours Good King Wenceslas, it is more likely that the king concerned was the husband of Elizabeth of Bohemia, daughter of James I. Next to the pub is the ornate **entrance** to the old brewery, established in 1720. It now leads to the peaceful OLD BREWERY MEWS, designed in 1973 by Dinerman Davison. The **brewery** building, which is now offices, was rebuilt in 1869 and has kept many of its original window openings (see plaque). **Nos. 6–7** are the site of Miss Noble's school, where Constable sent his daughters in the 1830s. There has been a bookshop in this stretch of the High Street for over 150 years. Here now is the High Hill Bookshop, which achieved some notoriety in recent years with its notice: 'Children of Progressive Parents Admitted only on Leads'.

Embedded in the wall across the road is an eighteenth-century **milestone** inscribed '3½ m from St Giles's Pound, 4 m from Holborn Bars' (the animal pound was near St Giles-in-the-Fields). **Nos. 1a–c** were built with **Essex Court** on the garden of the Trinity Presbyterian Church, which was pulled down in 1962 after a century of service. Maggie Richardson, who sold flowers at this corner for sixty years, is commemorated on the east wall with a flowery **plaque**, designed by Gillian Greenwood.

ROSSLYN HILL was earlier known as Red Lion Hill after an old pub on the south side. From the early nineteenth century the new name, at first Roslyn (*sic*) Street, commemorated the notorious Alexander Wedderburn, Earl of Rosslyn, who in 1801 moved from Branch Hill Lodge (q.v.) to a mansion in the Wedderburn Road area and renamed it Rosslyn House. On the north side, **Nos. 54–66** were re-built in 1890 with delightful florid facades. These include the initials of the dyer and the dairyman then at Nos. 66 and 62 respectively, and the proclamation of Dudman's Hampstead Borough Stores over No. 56, long a grocery but recently gallicised. On the site of these shops until 1880 was the oddly-named Chicken House, a Jacobean building, reputedly once a hunting lodge. This contained a remarkable stained glass window (reproduced in Park and elsewhere), showing portraits of James I and his favoured Duke of Buckingham, with a French inscription stating that they stayed the night here on 25 August 1619.

Below No. 54 is the entrance to PILGRIM'S PLACE, developed in the early nineteenth century and named after the Pilgrim family of Vane House: the three cottages were bought by **Rosslyn Hill Chapel** in 1918. This Unitarian Chapel, built by John Johnson in 1862 and enlarged in 1885, is near the site of a chapel for protestant dissenters dating back to 1691 (see Willoughby Road). Among the fine Victorian stained glass windows are works by William Morris, Burne-Jones and Henry Holiday, and in the chancel are two relief panels attributed to John Flaxman. In 1898 the chapel bought and demolished two shops in Rosslyn Hill to gain a proper entry from the main road. Their temperance campaigners also worried about the proximity of the **Rosslyn Arms**, which went up in 1869, the year after the Red Lion came down. Above **No. 40** is a cobbled cul-de-sac called ROSSLYN MEWS, which in the 1890s was a builder's yard for George Hart. The bank building of 1896, by Horace Field in Queen Anne style, is one of the few of this period on the DOE lists.

At the corner of Downshire Hill, the **police station**, which is No. 26½, was built in 1913 to designs by J. Dixon Butler, a disciple of Norman Shaw. Pevsner considered it 'oversize but very pretty'. At first glance **Nos. 22–24** appear to be Queen Anne houses, with two plaques saying 1702 to prove it. The DOE declares, however, that this was a mid eighteenth-century mansion, rebuilt as two houses in the mid nineteenth century, and that one plaque is a fake and the other imported from elsewhere. The latter includes the initials ZM, which may relate to Zechariah Morrell, an early eighteenth-century minister of Rosslyn Hill Chapel. In the late 1940s, the **Studio House** on the west of Hampstead Hill Gardens was the headquarters of the new Hampstead Artists Council, and **No. 12** on the east side was the home of leading cubist and vorticist David Bomberg, who is well represented at the Tate.

At the bottom of the hill, and currently at a low ebb, is **St Stephen's Church**, built in 1869 to the exuberant designs of Samuel Sanders Teulon. The site was part of the manorial waste called Hampstead Green and riddled with streams, so the foundations were never easy. But here Teulon, the rogue architect of over a hundred churches, created his *magnum opus*—and died, exhausted, soon after. On one Sunday in 1886, the church had 1,372 attendances. In 1977 it was made redundant and still faces an uncertain future, too expensive to demolish, even more costly to restore.

On the other side of Rosslyn Hill, **No. 11** was built in 1740, according to the owner, and in the late eighteenth century according to the DOE. Called Rosslyn Grove, the house may have been the Dower House of the Earl of Rosslyn, says the one, and manse of the Congregational Church in Lyndhurst Road, says the other. More certainly, this was the home until 1932 of Hancock Nunn, Hampstead's remarkable pioneer of social service: his name is little seen now except on a block of flats in Fellows Road.

Of the Victorian houses higher up the hill, **Nos. 15–41** were originally Mansfield Villas and **Nos. 43–53** Rosslyn Terrace. Above here the dried-up **drinking fountain** marks the site of the Red Lion inn, after which the old road was named. The pub was demolished in 1868 and replaced by a police station. This lasted until 1913, when No. 26½ was custom built for the constabulary.

At the entrance to VANE CLOSE, built in 1972, a red **plaque** asserts that 'Sir Harry Vane lived here' until his beheading in 1662. This apparent time-warp is due to the surprising survival of the plaque from old Vane House, which was demolished here in 1970. Sir Harry, the 'prince of paradoxes', tried to support both sides in the Civil War and was trusted by neither. He was, said Charles II, 'too dangerous a man to let live if we can honestly put him out of the way'. Sir Harry was arrested at his Hampstead home on a trumped-up charge of treason and marched to his death at the Tower of London. His house was taken in the 1740s by the famous theologian, Bishop Butler, and from 1781–95 by Admiral Matthew Barton. Accommodated mistakenly by previous local histories at Admiral's House (q.v.), Barton retired to Vane House after an exciting career. This included being shipwrecked naked on the Barbary coast and carried into slavery by the Moors. It was not until eighteen months later that he was ransomed by the British Government, who promptly courtmartialled him for the loss of his ship. For the last hundred years or so of its life, this house became the Royal Soldiers' Daughters Home, but they now have new premises at **No. 65**. The institution began in 1855 as the Crimean War ended, and after three years in Rosslyn House the girls were marched up the hill to Vane House, led by Prince Albert. The nearby MULBERRY CLOSE commemorates a fine old tree in the grounds of this historic mansion which, apart from a name plaque, has been lost without trace.

Connecting Rosslyn Hill and Fitzjohns Avenue is SHEPHERD'S WALK, a name said to derive from local land-owners called Shepherd. The **postal sorting office**, built in 1951, is on the site of St John's House, which in 1940 was, as the plaque notes, 'destroyed by enemy action'. This had previously been a boys' day school and a Cable and Wireless Training School.

The lane emerges in FITZJOHNS AVENUE, just above **Shepherd's Well**, which is now another dried-up drinking fountain but originally produced Hampstead's purest water. It is also the source of the River Tyburn, which later fills the lake in Regent's Park and flows past Buckingham Palace. The avenue was built in the 1870s over mainly manorial land and named after a Maryon Wilson estate in Essex. The northern, narrower stretch, which is the only part covered by this survey, followed a well-worn route for villagers or their paid water-carriers, using Shepherd's Well. Shown as Field Place on the 1832 map and as Greenhill Road on the first Ordnance Survey of 1866, it was not officially included in Fitzjohns Avenue until 1892.

Just above Shepherd's Walk is the entrance to **Fitzjohns Primary School**, founded in 1954. The handsome main building, however, dates from 1858, when it was erected as a school for the Royal Soldiers' Daughters. By 1951 it had become surplus to the daughters' requirements and was sold to the LCC. Higher up, **Henderson Court** was built in 1966 as old people's flats and named after a local worthy, Sir Vivian Henderson. The concrete family group in the courtyard was made by Mary Gorrara in her Steele's Road studio: she eventually had to knock a wall down to get it out. Before the last war, **No. 104** rang with strains of 'Frognal, Frognal, high on the hill', the school song of the prestigious Frognal School for Girls. In the 1920s, its ex-Roedean headmistresses were offering education 'on public school lines', including Swedish drill twice weekly. **No. 114** shows its date (1878) and the initials of its first occupant, William Huson Watts, a busy builder, who suitably called this house The Hive. **No. 116**, Monro House, was designed by Edward Ellis (with nautical crest) as the Royal Sailors' Daughters Home.

This institution, which originated at 99 Frognal after the Crimean War, offered asylum for one hundred girls, and education as domestic servants. The building was opened in 1869 by Prince Arthur of Connaught, who laid a memorial stone and planted a fir tree. Neither of these is visible now but note the bird's nest over the door. The home was closed in 1957 and converted to old people's flats, named after the home's long-serving secretary, F. R. D'O. Monro.

On the other side of the avenue, **No. 79** is known as Hyelm, which is a Hostel for Young Employees of Limited Means. Arthur West House was opened in 1975 (architect: Stefan Zins) and named after the founder of the original hostel in 1926: his portrait by Frank Salisbury hangs in the hall. At the corner with Arkwright Road, the harmonious **Field Court**, commemorating Field Place, was developed for the Council in 1978 by Pollard, Thomas and Edwards. This was locally called the 'Klondike site', after the three-fifths of an acre was sold in 1967 for £37,600 and resold five years later for five times that amount. **No. 75** was built in the early 1870s by T. K. Green for Paul Falconer Poole, RA, painter of historic subjects. This ambitious Gothic villa is called 'a good example of its kind' by the DOE, and 'crude, elephantine' by Pevsner. There is another architectural curiosity at **No. 73**, which has had an unremarkable window inserted by the mighty C. F. A. Voysey.

T. K. Green was the main architect of the Greenhill estate, on which ARKWRIGHT ROAD (derivation unknown) was a major development in the 1870s. **No. 1**, now part of St Anthony's School, Green designed for himself in what Andrew Saint has called 'Ruskinian Gothic'. **Nos. 2 and 4**, now St Godric's Secretarial College, were also by him, the latter for the then popular artist, F. W. Topham. **No. 9**, which is clearly by a different hand in 1874, was from 1909 the home of millionaire Sir Joseph Beecham, famous for his pill as well as for his son, Sir Thomas. This grand house, complete with a new wing added by Sir Joseph for a picture gallery, was bought in 1921 for £10,000 by the rich railway union, ASLEF, and has been its headquarters ever since. On the site of **Nos. 11a–f** was the home in the 1930s and 40s of Sir Geoffrey Keynes, brother of Maynard and polymath extraordinary. Apart from pioneering thyroid surgery (at New End Hospital) and blood transfusions, he was a noted bibliographer and expert on William Blake. The new houses here, as well as **Nos. 36a–e**, are by local architect L. J. Michaels.

The blue plaque on **No. 21** salutes Tobias Matthay, who lived here from 1902–9. It must be the only official plaque to a piano teacher, but the Matthay method, taught by him at the Royal Academy of Music for over fifty years, entitled him, as one critic said, to a 'prominent position in the pantheon of pianoforte pedagogues'. On the way down hill, note the dragon on the copper dome of **No. 28.** At the foot of the hill, **Camden Arts Centre** was built in 1897 as Hampstead's first Central Public Library. The site was more or less in the centre of the old borough. The building, designed in domestic Tudor style by Arnold Taylor, was twice bombed in the last war. The library transferred to Swiss Cottage in 1964.

Also on the Greenhill estate, ELLERDALE ROAD had its name approved in 1872, though the southern leg was called Manners Road until 1881. Like Arkwright,

Ellerdale sounds North Country but has no known derivation. **No. 24**, built as Briarlea in 1873, with *Vivat Veritas* over the door, came to life in 1898 with the new King Alfred's 'Co-Educational and Open Air' School. Their aim 'to develop the natural capacity of every individual', with no competitions or marks, and no religious instruction, appealed particularly to local artistic families such as the Farjeons and the Rothensteins. The school transferred to North End Road in 1921. On the east side, **No. 9** was the home of duettists Anne Ziegler and Webster Booth in the 1950s. **No. 12** offered Board Residence in the 1930s, under the title The Yellow Door, and with the curious slogan, 'Food You Remember, Beds You Forget'.

Nearby ELLERDALE CLOSE was developed in the mid 1930s and designed by Clough Williams Ellis. The first resident at **No. 1**, Beverley, was the journalistic author, Beverley Nichols, whose *Green Grows the City* described Hampstead and this house and garden—and the local fogs which, 'by the time they get to the top of the hill have shed much of their viciousness'. Several houses in Ellerdale Road have sunflowers on them, and **No. 6** is no exception: it also has its date (1875) and all the marks of a Norman Shaw house. In fact, the master architect built it for himself and lived here until his death in 1912. He is buried in the parish churchyard. During his residence here, he designed New Scotland Yard and the Piccadilly Hotel and several local houses, including 61 Fitzjohns Avenue. In the 1930s, the house became Hampstead Towers Hotel, but it is now a seminary run by the Sisters of St Marcellina. Next door, **No. 2**, is another defiantly Gothic house, with delightful detail, built for

himself about 1890 by the energetic T. K. Green. It has been DOE listed 'for curiosity value'.

Though not a main road in the sense of a major thoroughfare—and all traffic should really be barred here—CHURCH ROW is certainly the best show-piece in Hampstead. Nearly all the houses are of early eighteenth-century origin, with flush-framed windows, and though many have been rebuilt or refaced they have kept up their period appearances with decorative fanlights, canopies and wrought iron work. The Town Improvements did not improve the east end of the street, where old houses disappeared and in 1898, **Gardnor Mansions** arrived (the Gardnor family owned land here), the first blocks of flats in central Hampstead. Among the flat-dwellers in the 1920s was Margaret Llewelyn Davies (q.v.) and, in the 1930s, Gracie Fields.

The narrow **No. 5**, which was weatherboarded in the late eighteenth century, was recently reconverted to a residence from the offices of Shepherd the builder: the asking price in 1982 was £100,000. Around 1800, **No. 8** was the home of two famous but now forgotten writers—Mrs Barbauld, whose husband was a minister at Rosslyn Hill Chapel, and her niece, Lucy Aikin, who loved Hampstead because 'neighbours do not think it necessary, as in the provinces, to force their acquaintance upon you'. **No. 9** was a Girls' Reformatory School in the 1860s, and a Field Lane Industrial School for Girls in the 1890s. The writer Nicholas Mosley, Lord Ravensdale, son of Sir Oswald, lived here in recent years. **No. 12**, which is late eighteenth-century, was for long the home of Geoffrey Hutchinson, QC, later Lord Ilford, who successfully fought for the Heath and Old Hampstead until his death here in 1974. Sir Norman Collins, who lived at **Mulberry House** at the west end of the street, left the BBC to champion commercial broadcasting, for which he coined the euphemism Independent Television: he also wrote the popular novel, *London Belongs to Me.* Up to the end of the last century, a toll had to be paid at a gate across Church Row, at its junction with Frognal Gardens, as right of way through to Frognal belonged to the Old Mansion (q.v.). **No. 14** has been the vicarage of St John-at-Hampstead since the 1930s. **No. 15** is a remarkably harmonious addition to the Georgian terraces: it was erected only in 1924.

The present **Parish Church** was built in 1747 by John Sanderson on the site of a medieval church, which had become unsuitable and unsafe for Hampstead's burgeoning population. As early as 1710, the congregation had been petitioning Parliament for repairs or replacement, as they could not 'come to Divine Service without Apparent Hazard of their lives'. The new church was dedicated to St John the Evangelist: its predecessor had been St Mary's. After various extensions by Robert Hesketh, the church was enlarged and reorientated in 1878, to plans by F. P. Cockerell. As a result, the chancel and altar are at the west end, an arrangement not much found except in Hampstead and St Peter's in Rome. The church has some fine stained glass by Clayton and Bell, and memorials to Keats and other local celebrities. The churchyard is full of famous names, but only four graves are DOE listed—John Constable, George du Maurier, Sir Walter Besant and John Harrison. The last-named, who invented the marine chronometer, had no known local connection but, like many Londoners, chose to be buried in these rural surroundings. The entrance gates were brought in 1747 (see plaque) from the Duke of Chandos's residence, Canons Park in Edgware, where Handel composed his 'Chandos Anthems',

On the south side of Church Row, **No. 17** was the home in 1909 of H. G. Wells—or rather of his wife and sons, as the author had just eloped with Amber Reeves (see 44 Downshire Hill). He returned to the family in 1910, and is shown in the local directory of that year as a JP, but his two novels published in 1910 (*The History of Mr Polly* and *The New Machiavelli*) were both about husbands fleeing unfortunate marriages. The Wells family left Church Row for Essex in 1912. **No. 18** has a plaque to J. J. Park, who wrote the first history of Hampstead in 1814, and to his father, who must have helped him, as J. J. was only nineteen at the time. **No. 19** was the home, until his death in 1979, of Sir Frank Soskice, later Lord Stow Hill, who succeeded Henry Brooke as Home Secretary when Socialists took over from Tories in 1964: he was grandson of Ford Madox Brown.

New trees were presented to Church Row in 1876 by three architects living at **Nos. 20, 24 and 26** respectively, Thomas Garner, G. F. Bodley and George Gilbert Scott junior. Another architect in Scott's office, Temple Moore, helped to plant them. Two other noted artists worked at No. 20—Henry Holiday (q.v.) in the 1890s, and Randolph Schwabe in the 1930s and 40s: he was then principal of the Slade School. **Nos. 24–28** are, according to the DOE, 'early nineteenth-century, refaced later nineteenth century in Georgian style'. No. 24 has a *fleur de lys* cut in the first floor brickwork, which was the trade mark of C. B. King, a builder who specialised in neo-Georgian work in Hampstead (see Elm Row). His offices were at No. 28. G. G. Scott junior's son, (Sir) Giles, was born at No. 26 in 1880. At the age of twenty-two he won the competition to design the Liverpool Anglican Cathedral. Later celebrities here include William Rothenstein, whose son (Sir) John went to King Alfred's, Lord Alfred Douglas and wife (1907–10) and, in the 1950s, Ludovic Kennedy and Moira Shearer. No. 27 was the home of George du Maurier (1870–74) whose son, (Sir) Gerald, was born here in 1873, and of the folk song-and-dance expert, Cecil Sharp (1915–18).

No. 28 deserves a book to itself. A Catholic school in the 1850s gives way to a Home for the Rescue of Young Women in the '60s, which is replaced (or renamed) in the '70s by a Female Servants' Home. The builders move in by the '90s, that is C. B. King's office, and are soon joined by various artists including Muirhead Bone, who in 1910 lets his flat (without bathroom) to Compton Mackenzie at £4 per month. The author describes in *Octave 4* how an etching of Bone's he found in the flat gave him the title of one of his earliest successes, *Sinister Street*. Finally, from 1908 this was the office of the Women's Cooperative Guild and Margaret Llewelyn Davies, whose visitors included Leonard and Virginia Woolf. The latter often came to the 'immaculate and moral heights of Hampstead' and admired its 'uncompromising and highminded' inhabitants, many of whom she must have found among the delights of Church Row.

The Vale of Health, about 1863, when the Hampstead Heath Hotel (right) was built. The chapel-like building is the Athenaeum Hall. *From an unidentified periodical of the 1860s.*

The Outskirts

AT the top of Hampstead Hill, where on a clear day there are breathtaking views to east and west, NORTH END WAY leads down to the borough border. This is the highest point in North London, 440 feet above sea level, and about 20 feet higher than the cross of St Paul's. The clumps of bushes on the south side were planted partly to discourage the donkey touts of fifty years ago. Here they had their stands and offered rides on some of the 'hundred Hampstead donkeys'. It was George du Maurier who nicknamed **Whitestone Pond** 'Ponds Asinorum'. Among the bushes south of the pond, in the shadow of the new radio **aerial**, is the old white **milestone** after which the pond is named. The faded inscription reads on one side '4½ miles from Holborn Bars', and on the other 'IV miles from St Giles's Pound'. Ramps at either end of the pond show that horse-drawn vehicles used to drive right through this rain-water pond, but most of the paddlers are now two-legged. Below the road to the east is the disused **Pinfold** or cattle pound, which dates from 1787.

The **flagstaff** flying the GLC flag marks the site of the Armada beacon, one of a chain of signal fires in Elizabethan times, when a Spanish invasion was threatened. 'High on bleak Hampstead's swarthy moor, they started for the north', wrote Macaulay in *The Lay of the Spanish Armada*. The first flagstaff was erected by the Lord of the Manor about 1845 and flew his flag (the cross of St George) whenever a Manorial Court was being held. The **Old Court House** is the name of the house to the north, but there is no evidence of courts being held here, or that this was, according to one story, where Judge Jeffreys 'persecuted his prisoners'. The house was built in the 1780s by the owner of the adjoining tavern, where Manorial Courts were in fact held every Christmas, and in the nineteenth century became the Manor Estate Office. The Lord of the Manor also lodged here on his rare visits to Hampstead. Earlier called Heath View and Earlsmead, the Old Court House was converted to old people's flats in the 1960s.

Jack Straw's Castle, which can claim to be the highest pub in London and to have been patronised by the highest in the land, is also a misnomer. The notorious Jack Straw of the Peasants' Revolt of 1381 almost certainly never came here (nor did his leader, Wat Tyler, after whom a bar is named), and there never was a castle. But by 1713, when the tavern's name was first mentioned, there had been a revival of interest in the semi-legendary peasant rebel, and at least two plays were written about him. The pub was badly bombed in the last war and rebuilt in 1962 by Raymond Erith, with a comically castellated front. The main bar is named after Dick Turpin, another semi-legendary association, but the real-life Charles Dickens, who came here often and praised the chops, is no longer commemorated.

The **war memorial**, dating from 1922, was extended in 1953 and moved from the middle of the road to ground donated by the owners of **Heath House**. This early eighteenth-century mansion was bought in 1790 by Samuel Hoare, the Quaker banker, whose family took a squirely interest in Hampstead for over a century. They were instrumental in starting schools, relieving the poor, building churches and saving the Heath. They also entertained William Wilberforce here to further his anti-slavery campaign and discussed prison reform with Elizabeth Fry. The house got its present name when taken in 1888 by newspaper proprietor, Sir Algernon Borthwick, later Baron Glenesk. He was succeeded here by the Guinness family, one of whom became the Earl of Iveagh in 1919 and moved to Ken Wood. Heath House, which then passed to his third son, created Baron Moyne in 1932, has not surprisingly been called 'a veritable breeding place for the peerage'.

A cluster of cottages called Littleworth grew up behind Jack Straw's Castle in the eighteenth century, but by 1800 the smallholders had been swept away by a wave of Whig aristocracy. The new residents included Lady Crewe, Lady Camelford and Lord William Grenville, leader in 1806/7 of the government which abolished the slave trade. The villas, which grew to prestigious size, were mostly destroyed by a parachute mine in 1941 and their grounds added to the Heath. Some of their garden **trees** can still be seen between the pub and Inverforth House. HILLBROW, which led to a villa of that name, now only leads to a car park.

Inverforth House is on the site of a smaller house called The Hill, which was given by Samuel Hoare to his son in 1807, when the latter married Elizabeth Fry's sister. The black plaque records that John Gurney Hoare, who was born here in 1810, took a leading part in the battle to save the Heath from development. The Hill was bought in 1906 by William Lever, later Lord Leverhulme, the son of a Bolton grocer who made his fortune from Sunlight Soap. He rebuilt the house, added a wing or two (one for his art gallery), acquired two neighbouring properties, Cedar Lawn (its cedar is visible from the road) and Heath Lodge, had new grounds designed by Thomas Mawson, and built the pergola walks. The Heath Lodge estate, now **The Hill Garden**, was unfortunately separated from the rest of the property by a public footpath, but all Leverhulme's powers and riches could not buy him this right-of-way. Despite many national and local benefactions, he died in 1924 worth fifty-seven million pounds. Lord Inverforth, the shipping magnate, lived at The Hill from the following year and in 1955 bequeathed it to Manor House Hospital. The road past **Inverforth Close** leads to the charming Hill Garden now open to the public: the aluminium sculpture near the entrance is by Stephen Gilbert.

The **cutting** in North End Way, probably dating from the 1730s, was famous for its Gibbet Elms, which stood just to the north of The Hill for many years. Here in 1673 was hanged the villainous highwayman, Francis Jackson, and his skeleton was left dangling in chains for another eighteen years. The last of these elms was blown down as recently as 1907. The hamlet of North End is presumed to be the Sandgate mentioned in the charter of 986 (Sandy

Heath is very near), and from Tudor times it is often referred to as Wildwood Corner. This is the name in Camden's *Britannia* of 1695.

North End has long been famous for its two pubs, both of which are mentioned in the Holborn Register of 1730. **The Bull and Bush**, popularised by Florrie Forde's song, developed from a farmhouse reputedly built about 1645. The young William Hogarth lived here and laid out the gardens, which became a popular attraction of the tavern. Gainsborough, who drank here with Reynolds and Garrick, called it 'a delightful little snuggery'. Of the many theories about the name, the most likely derives the 'bull' from the farm and the 'bush' from the ivy bush that was a tavern sign. The present building dates largely from 1924. **The Hare and Hounds**, which was twice bombed in 1940 and existed for a time in five linked caravans, was rebuilt in 1968.

Across the borough boundary and above the entrance to **Golders Hill Park**, which was added to the Heath in 1899, is **Ivy House**, where ballerina Anna Pavlova lived from 1912–31. Golders Hill was saved by public subscription and enough money was raised to buy an additional patch for the Heath opposite the Bull and Bush. This was the site of an old terrace called Ambridge Cottages, two of which have survived. One has kept the name of the terrace and the other, long the home of the quizzical Nicholas Parsons, is known as **Briar Cottage**. The western leg of SANDY ROAD starts near here and soon comes to **No. 9**, which was the North End School. This was built by John Gurney Hoare in 1849 and managed by his youngest daughter, Margaret. The bell is still under the eaves and a homily about leading a child 'in the way he should go' is still visible on the roof line.

Further west, the road turns into a track and passes the **Leg o'Mutton Pond**, the name descriptive of its shape. The reservoir was made by some parish paupers in 1825 as part of a job creation scheme devised by Mr Hankin, a Poor Relief Supervisor. The project was soon known as Hankin's Folly. To the east of the pond a **mesolithic site** has recently been excavated, and considerable information unearthed about Early Man in Hampstead. This was evidently the camp site of some forest hunters in 7000 BC. The narrow HEATH PASSAGE leads back to the main road. In the 1950s, **No. 4** was the studio of Boris Anrep, who designed the new mosaic floor for the National Gallery foyer in this period. The continuation of Sandy Road on the east side of North End Way has been called NORTH END since 1942. **Nos. 1 and 3** are an early eighteenth-century pair, and **Wildwood Lodge** is a mid ninteenth-century Gothic *cottage orné*. This last house, which has been owned by the same family fore over a hundred years, was sold in 1869 by Queen Victoria's dentist.

In NORTH END AVENUE, a plaque on the gate to new **Pitt House** records its remarkable predecessor, demolished in 1952. Variously known as Wildwoods and North End Place, the house was used in 1767 for convalescence by the Prime Minister, William Pitt, Earl of Chatham. He was so sick in body and mind that he shut himself away in a top room and refused to see anyone: all his food was served through a hatch. George III was so worried that at one point he threatened to visit Pitt at North End himself. From 1905–8, this was the home of Harold Harmsworth, later Lord Rothermere, and from

1914 of the Fleming family, whose famous sons, Ian and Peter, were brought up here. To the south, the grounds of Pitt House have been absorbed in the Heath, including an old **arch**. This was presumably the entrance to the property before the cutting was made, when North End Avenue was the main road.

Across the avenue, the uncottagey **Byron Cottage**, which is not listed, is mainly eighteenth-century. This was known as Myrtle Lodge or Myrtlewood until Lady Byron came to live here in 1908. She was the wife of the ninth Lord Byron known as 'red-nosed George', and only distantly related to the poet. He was one of a succession of rich husbands for this ex-chorus-girl, whom Churchill described as 'the modern Boadicea'. In 1924 she married Sir Robert Houston, a shipping magnate and, as Lady Houston, was noted as one of the wealthiest women in the country. Among other causes, she poured money into the struggling British aircraft industry, which greatly helped the development of the Spitfire engine. This is why one of her biographers called her 'the Woman who Won the War'. To the north **No. 23**, North End Lodge (also unlisted), has been dated about 1760 but the local artist, Mary Hill, who lived there a century ago, claimed that part was as old as Queen Anne.

At the corner opposite Byron Cottage, an old **boundary stone** dated 1833 appears to have slipped a bit, as the borough boundary is about a hundred yards to the north. In this direction are the totally tile-hung **Wildwood** and **No. 15**, an eighteenth-century farmhouse divided up in 1809. Across the road, **No. 19** was built in the 1950s by the young architect, Michael Ventris, famous in archaeological circles for having decoded the Cretan hieroglyphics known as Linear B.

To the north is **Wildwood Terrace**, architecturally unremarkable except for the residence at **No. 2** from 1936–83 of Sir Nikolaus Pevsner. The indefatigable art historian, who has opened so many eyes to the joys and quirks of architecture, will be best remembered by his Domesday Survey of *The Buildings of England* in forty-seven volumes. Incidentally, this project could not have been completed without the financial support of the Leverhulme Trust (see above). Behind here is a Victorian terrace called WILDWOOD GROVE, first mentioned in the 1873 Directory. In the 1950s, **No. 5** was the home of actor-manager Donald Wolfit, whose parts at this period ranged from Tamburlaine at the Old Vic to Captain Hook at the Scala.

In all the wilds of North End, the most picturesque place is **Wyldes** itself, bestriding the border of Hampstead and Hendon. The two houses, now called Old Wyldes and Wyldes, were respectively the home farmhouses and barn of the 340-acre estate: the farmland has been absorbed by Hampstead Heath Extension and Hampstead Garden Suburb. In medieval times, the estate was owned by the leper hospital of St James (where St James's Palace now stands), and for 370 years it belonged to Eton College. From about 1785–1854 the farm was let to the Collins family and took their name, though it was variously known as Heath Farm and Wildwood Farm. From 1824–28, the young artist, John Linnell, was lodging here with his family and was often visited by his future son-in-law, Samuel Palmer, and by the aged William Blake, whom Linnell had befriended. A joint plaque on Old Wyldes now commemorates this friendship. Dickens was another distinguished lodger here in 1837, when recovering from the death of his sister-in-law, Mary Hogarth. The farmers had gone by 1884, when Charlotte Wilson lived here and started a revolutionary study circle called the Hampstead Historic Club. This was not concerned with local history, but with Fabian ideology, and Wyldes became a meeting place for Shaw, Sidney Webb, E. Nesbit and other radical thinkers. In 1906, the whole property was taken over by the Hampstead Garden Suburb Trust, partly as its estate office and partly as the home of its chief architect, Sir Raymond Unwin. A plaque on Wyldes notes his residence here from 1906–40, but the family owned the house until 1967, when it was sold up and divided into its present handsome state.

On the south-east side of Sandy Heath, SPANIARDS ROAD leads to another of Hampstead's border settlements. The ancient road, which is first named by the 1866 Ordnance Survey, is now higher than the surrounding Heath because of extensive sand quarrying on either side. In 1866–67, for instance, a quarter of an acre of sand and ballast was sold by the Lord of the Manor to the Midland Railway. Much sand was also removed for filling sandbags in two world wars. The street name derives from its climax, **the Spaniards Inn**, which is technically in the borough of Barnet, as the **boundary stones** show. (The 1799 stone marked FP means Finchley Parish, now part of Barnet). Tradition has it that Spain's ambassador to the court of James I had a house on this site, and that his valet later started an inn. More certainly, here was the lodge house and toll-gate for the Bishop of London's park, which stretched to the top of Highgate Hill (site of another toll-gate): the colony was then known as Parkgate. The eighteenth-century **toll-house**, which happily still slows down the traffic, was rescued by local conservationists in 1967: its restoration reaped a Civic Trust Award. The present pub building dates from the early eighteenth century, when the Spa brought rich custom for the tavern and its pleasure gardens.

In the Gordon Riots of 1780, Kenwood House, then occupied by the Earl of Mansfield, was saved from destruction—unlike his town house—when the landlord of the Spaniards offered the rioters unlimited refreshment at the inn. This delayed them sufficiently for a message to be sent summoning the military. The inn was popular with Dickens, who portrayed it in *Pickwick* and, some say, with Dick Turpin, not to mention Black Bess. Some even remember the highwayman's very own pistol being fired nightly as a closing time signal.

Straddling the borough borders, and therefore liable to two separate rate demands, is **Erskine House**, adapted from the wing of an old house of that name which was demolished in 1923. The original eighteenth-century house was the home in the 1760s of John Sanderson, architect of the parish church, and from 1788 of Lord Erskine. This forensic genius, who even won the riotous Gordon's acquittal, with Lord Mansfield in the seat of judgement, expanded his garden across the road by building a tunnel: the far end can still be seen from the Heath. Erskine, who lived here until 1821, called his property **Evergreen Hill**, which is now the name of the house next door. To add to the confusion, this was once part of the adjoining **Heath End House**, which dates from about 1788. The latter was the home of the arctic explorer, Sir William Parry (1790–1855), who brought a pair of whale jaws here for a garden arch, and from 1889 of Canon and Mrs Barnett: she is better known as Dame Henrietta Barnett, prime promoter of Hampstead Garden Suburb. Now commemorated by a blue plaque, the Barnetts renamed the house St Jude's Cottage, after his Whitechapel parish, and turned old Erskine House into a convalescent home. In 1895 they lent their cottage to the American painter, Whistler, whose wife died here. The successful novelist, Sir Hall Caine, converted all this property to his liking in 1923, and stayed here until his death in 1931.

At the entrance to SPANIARDS END, a large mansion called The Firs was divided in the 1950s into **The White House** and **The Chantry**, with an unexpected extra called **Casa Maria**. The latter was adapted from the billiard room of The Firs and in a Spanish style, as this seemed appropriate to the area. The main house was built in 1734 by John Turner, a rich draper (Park says tobacconist) of Fleet Street, who is credited with building the sandy road from here to North End, which still exists. Not so longeval was the clump of firs he planted near his house, but at least these were frequently recorded by artists, including Constable. All the desirable eighteenth-century **cottages** in Spaniards End were converted from the stables and garden sheds of The Firs.

On the other side of Spaniards Road, in several acres of grounds, is a mansion still known as **The Elms**, but which was recently St Columba's Hospital. The property was sold to a sheik in 1981 for over two and a half million pounds. The house, built about 1875, is on the historic site of Mother Huff's Tea Gardens, which flourished here for fifty years from 1678. The art dealer, Sir Joseph Joel Duveen, who added the Turner Wing to the Tate Gallery, lived at The Elms from 1894 to 1908: his monogram is over the gate.

Traditionally THE VALE OF HEALTH was a place of refuge for seventeenth-century citizens fleeing the Great Plague of London. But tradition can be an ass. The name is not found anywhere until 1801, and at the time of the plague this area was an unhealthy swamp. It was not until 1777 that the vale was drained by the Hampstead Water Company, and the **pond** built as a new reservoir. (The other Hampstead ponds were made in Tudor times.) The area was then known as Hatch's Bottom, after its only inhabitant, Samuel Hatch, and it seems likely that the Company coined the new name thinking that their customers would not want their water from a place with such an insanitary name.

To the north of the pond is a small **fairground**, for long owned by the Gray family, who also ran the Vale of Health Hotel. This towering tavern, on the site of **Spencer House** (architect: L. J. Michaels), was built in 1863 but was not a success. Parts were let out as factory, shops, Salvation Army barracks and studios. The artist Henry Lamb worked here from 1912–24: his portrait of Lytton Strachey, with a vaguely Vale background, is in the Tate. Stanley Spencer, after whom the flats are named, was here from 1924–27, mostly painting his *Cookham Resurrection*. The studio windows had to be removed to get the picture out (it is also in the Tate), as it was too big to take down the stairs.

To the west is **1 Byron Villas**, where a blue plaque salutes a brief appearance by D. H. Lawrence in 1915. This was the only London home that he and Frieda had:

she came to be near the children of her first marriage, and he to see the publication of *The Rainbow*. The novel caused outrage and was banned, and this, together with a zeppelin raid they viewed from the Heath (described in his *Kangaroo*), hurried their departure to Cornwall. In the few months they were here, though, they held court in the Vale, with courtiers including Bertrand Russell, Aldous Huxley and Ottoline Morrell. Byron Villas were built in 1905 to replace a second Vale of Health Hotel from the 1860s, which also had a chequered career. Next door, the **Athenaeum** flats were built about 1960, on the site of an odd, chapel-like building, which at times housed a drinking club and at others the Salvation Army. Beyond the mini-spinney outside these flats is a **noticeboard** with a useful map of the Vale. There are no street names in the colony, and the GLC's attempt in 1966 to introduce names associated with Constable were rebuffed by the residents. To the south, is **Hollycroft**, with a blue plaque to the social historians, J. L. and Barbara Hammond, who lived here from 1906–13. This was also the home from 1931 of Norman Bentwich, professor of international law, and of his wife, Helen, one-time chairman of the LCC and author of the only history of the Vale of Health, first published in 1968.

Back north, another blue plaque on **Villas on the Heath** (not to be confused with Heath Villas) records the brief residence here in 1912 of (Sir) Rabindranath Tagore. The following year, this Indian poet and mystic received the Nobel Prize for Literature, the first Asian to do so, and in 1915 he was knighted. This last honour he resigned four years later in protest against British policy in the Punjab. To the east of this block, the early nineteenth-century

Woodbine Cottage was bought by Compton Mackenzie in 1937. He lived here off and on for six years, writing *The Four Winds of Love* and finding 'village life half an hour from Piccadilly Circus was a continuous refreshment and stimulus'.

All the houses to the north are early nineteenth-century, and most of them claim to have been the residence of the poet, Leigh Hunt (see below). **Hunt Cottage** is no exception, though it was called Rose Cottage when the impecunious Harmsworth family stayed here from 1870–73. The youthful Alfred and Harold, later to be press barons, were delighted to have George Jealous, editor of the *Ham and High*, as a near neighbour: he lived at **No. 1 Villas on the Heath**. Jealous is said to have greatly inspired the future Lord Northcliffe with the gift of a toy printing set. It was another editor, Ernest Rhys of the Everyman Library, who changed the name to Hunt Cottage while living there in the 1890s. **South Villa** has a home-made plaque to Leigh Hunt on its rear wall. **North Villa** may one day have a plaque to pianist Alfred Brendel, who lived here in the 1970s. **Vale Cottage** was Stella Gibbons's home in 1927–30. She wrote much of *Cold Comfort Farm* at her next Hampstead address, 67 Fitzjohns Avenue. At the end of the road, **The Gables** are marked 1883 and have a healthy outlook, but John Middleton Murry (q.v.), who lived at No. 1a in the 1920s, was so ill that he called the area The Vale of Sickness.

Leigh Hunt came to the Vale of Health in 1815 and probably to **Vale Lodge**, at the north end of the hamlet. He wanted to recuperate from two years in gaol for slandering the Prince Regent, a deed which made him so popular that his time in prison was a triumph. But his fame followed him to the Vale and his literary circle increased. Keats first came to Hampstead to call on him here in 1816, and Shelley entertained his many children by sailing paper boats on the pond. The Hunt family finally left the Vale in 1821 and joined the migration of poets to Italy. Among much later inhabitants of Vale Lodge have been Edgar Wallace, Sir Leon Bagrit and Sir Paul Chambers, the latter two in the 1950s; both are mentioned elsewhere in this book. It is worth exploring the narrow passage behind Vale Lodge to see the back of Rose Cottage and the picturesque, weather-boarded **Old Cottage**, listed as early nineteenth-century but looking much older. Up another alley to the west is **Chestnut Cottage**, dated about 1812 and for long the home of chimney sweeps.

Much has changed in the Vale of Health in its two centuries of development but, as in the rest of the surrounding area, much remains to surprise and delight the resident or visitor who wanders the streets of Hampstead.

MAIN SOURCES

Books

F. E. Baines: *Records of the Manor, Parish and Borough of Hampstead* (Whitaker/Hewetson 1890).

Thomas J. Barratt: *The Annals of Hampstead* (Black 1912, Lionel Leventhal 1972)

Helen Bentwich: *The Vale of Health* (High Hill Press 1968, Camden History Society 1977)

Mary Hill: *Hampstead in Light and Shade* (Baines & Scarsbrook, 1938, 1945)

W. Howitt: *The Northern Heights* (Longmans 1869)

C. W. Ikin: *Hampstead Heath* (GLC 1971)

J. Kennedy: *The Manor and Parish Church of Hampstead* (Mayle 1906)

Anna Maxwell: *Hampstead: Its Historic Houses, Its Literary and Artistic Associations* (James Clarke & Co. 1912)

Mavis and Ian Norrie (Ed.): *The Book of Hampstead* (High Hill Press 1968)

E. F. Oppé: *Hampstead–A London Town* (pub. by author 1951)

J. J. Park: *The Topography and Natural History of Hampstead* (Nichols, Son and Bentley, 1814, 1818)

Nikolaus Pevsner: *The Buildings of England–London except   the Cities of London and Westminster* (Penguin 1952)

G. W. Potter: *Hampstead Wells* (Bell 1904, Carlile House 1978)

G. W. Potter: *Random Recollections of Hampstead* (Eyre & Spottiswoode 1907)

F. M. L. Thompson: *Hampstead, Building a Borough 1650–1964* (Routledge & Kegan Paul 1974)

Edward Walford: *Old and New London*, Vol. V (Cassell c.1880)

Caroline A. White: *Sweet Hampstead and its Associations* (Elliot, Stock 1900, 1903)

The Hampstead Annuals 1897–1906 (Mayle)

Maps of Hampstead

1746	Rocque	1864	Daw
1762	Ellis	1866	Ordnance Survey
1803	Goodwin	1891	Lowe
1814	Newton	1895	Ordnance Survey
1835	Cruchley	1915	Ordnance Survey
1847	Lee	1934	Ordnance Survey
1862	Weller	1953	Ordnance Survey

Other Sources

52nd List of Buildings of Special Architectural or Historic Interest (Department of Environment 1974, with additions)

Blue Plaques on Houses of Historic Interest (GLC 1976, with additions)

Who's Who and *Who Was Who* (Black)

Dictionary of National Biography (OUP)

The Hampstead and Highgate Express (from 1872)

Camden's Local History Collection at Swiss Cottage and Holborn Libraries

Camden History Review Nos. 1–10

LCC Street Lists and GLC Street Naming Section

Exhibition Catalogues of Hampstead Artists' Council

INDEX

Bold type shows the names of streets in the survey and the main entry for each street